Character in Crisis

Edited by J. H. Hexter

PRIEST AND REVOLUTIONARY

PRIEST AND
REVOLUTIONARY

LAMENNAIS AND THE DILEMMA
OF FRENCH CATHOLICISM

Peter N. Stearns

HARPER & ROW, PUBLISHERS

NEW YORK, EVANSTON, AND LONDON

FIRST EDITION

LIBRARY OF CONGRESS CATALOG CARD NUMBER: 66–20760

B-R

St 595/250/4/25/67

For Duncan

CONTENTS

PRIEST AND REVOLUTIONARY

CHAPTER I

INTRODUCTION

After the fall of Napoleon relations between the Catholic Church and French politics and society entered a decisive new stage. For twenty-five years the French Church had been embattled, facing first the hostility of the revolution and then the more subtle controls of Napoleon. Now it could establish solid contacts with the state and, hopefully, regain some of the ground it had lost in society. Many churchmen thought that stability and normalcy, defined in prerevolutionary terms, had returned. But this was not the case; both state and society had changed. The currents of the revolution still ran strong. The question remained: What adjustment could the Church make to the revolutionary heritage? Could it accept a strong state, active in, say, education? Could it meet the growing demand for freedom of thought, of the press, of religion itself? Could it deal with a society increasingly urbanized, in which the social problems of early industrialization were already being felt? These were the leading issues for the Church. That many churchmen sought to ignore them simply added to the problem.

A number of Catholics saw that times had changed. Their leader, until 1834, was Hugues-Félicité Robert de La Mennais, a priest. Lamennais was to change his views in many ways during this period, but always his central concern was

1

the need to combine religion and the new society for the benefit of both. His efforts led him from a novel conservatism to flaming liberalism and even socialism. They brought him and the French Church to a crisis between 1830 and 1834, in which basic positions had to be defined on both sides. These definitions fixed the orientation of the Church, even outside of France, for many decades. They revealed much about the Church and French society. This same process of definition revealed much about Lamennais.

Lamennais, a passionate man, was convinced of his infallible intuition. As a prophet, he saw clearly the shape of things to come. He was a democrat as well, a man who looked to the people as a whole in an age in which democracy was rare. He was a man capable of attracting intense loyalty from some of the leading figures of the period and capable of returning loyalty with deep friendship. Lamennais also hated deeply and could see persecution at every turn. A frail man, often wracked by illness, he lived for his dreams of a Christian society that would be perfect.

This essay traces the interaction between the intense figure of Lamennais and the Church in France. It focuses on the years of crisis, 1830–1834. The key to the crisis was the Revolution of 1830, which Lamennais had long predicted. The revolution, although limited, revealed clearly that the old regime was dead. The Church would have to make positive adjustments, and Lamennais tried to ensure that these adjustments would be both explicit and radical. In this crisis anticlerical liberals had to deal with a clerical liberal, a man who claimed in Christianity political and social principles more radical than many of theirs. The Church encountered an unwanted revolutionary in its own ranks. Lamennais sought to wed the Church to the principles of revolution. Yet he could not win the revolutionaries to his cause and he certainly could not win the Church. It is possible that his efforts, by forcing a full statement of positions, created a

bigger gap between Church and revolution than was necessary. It is more probable that he simply made explicit an
inevitable tension.

This essay is a study in failure. The Church, quite under-
standably, could not choose the path that Lamennais had
marked out. Yet Lamennais was right about the broad lines
of future development. He was right that the Church would
lose ground steadily if it did not come to grips with modern
society. Many of his views were to be taken up again later,
in the twentieth century and even in the present day, as the
Church sought to cope with a society born of many revolutions. Perhaps, as has been suggested, Lamennais was simply
too far ahead of his own times.

For Lamennais, too, the period was a tragic one. The
focus of his whole life was in question. His financial position
was broken by the expenses of his campaign. His friends
deserted him. He had influence still, but his earlier popularity now waned. Increasingly he saw himself as a lonely
prophet, sure of the ultimate success of his ideas, but in the
meantime persecuted and abandoned.

The tragedy of Lamennais is a fascinating subject in itself,
for this is an individual of no small creative power. Beyond
this, through Lamennais one can grasp the real dilemma of
the Church in modern times. The crisis occurred in France,
for here the forces of revolution were strongest; but the confrontation of Church and revolution was to be repeated all
over Europe. Some positive elements did emerge. The Belgian Church in this period applied Mennaisian principles to
Church-state problems, with fruitful results. Even in France
the effort to accommodate Church to revolution was not
abandoned, though it required more flexibility on the part of
the Church than Lamennais' ideas permitted. From this
period, in part due to Lamennais' efforts, a persistent liberal
and socially-oriented Catholic movement emerged within
the Church. This movement was important, though not

dominant, in the remainder of the nineteenth century. In the twentieth, changes in Church politics and the rise of Christian democracy as a major political force have at least re-echoed the impassioned Breton priest.

CHAPTER II

———❦———

LAMENNAIS AND THE CHURCH
TO 1815

In the quarter-century before 1815 the Church in France and
to an extent in the rest of Europe had undergone a major
transformation. The changes, almost entirely imposed from
without, were all the more shattering because of the Church's
need to be a conservative body. The revolution altered the
political position of the Church, permanently in France and
temporarily even in Rome. Beyond this, Church doctrines
were under intellectual attack from the rationalist ideas of
the Enlightenment. In France particularly, the Church was
losing its hold on wide segments of the population; a process
of de-Christianization was occurring. In the Church's attempt to deal with this multiple crisis, there was a temptation to concentrate on political problems first, because they
were easiest to grasp and had been introduced so suddenly.
But ultimately all the problems had to be faced. The Church
had to come to grips with some of the essential features of
the modern world.

The Church before 1789 had been a privileged political
body. Its lands in France were exempt from taxation, though
the clergy annually voted a relatively small payment in lieu
of taxation. Members of the clergy were not subject to civil

5

jurisdiction for many crimes; special ecclesiastical courts existed instead. The Church kept most public records, such as those of marriages and deaths. It controlled the educational system, from primary schools through the university level. It controlled charity functions. It had powerful, though not overwhelming, influence over the state itself, with many individual prelates serving as ministers of state and as leaders of the provincial states general. The clergy as a whole was regarded as the first of the three estates of the nation. From the state the Church could obtain some protection against irreligious or un-Catholic writings and doctrines, though the protection was ineffective. There were many cases of censorship, destruction of books, and persecutions of Protestants in the eighteenth century.

At the same time, the Church was dependent on the state. The French Church operated under a Gallican constitution, in which the state was a more decisive authority than the pope in Rome. The government made all the major appointments to the Church. Through this power the state could influence even doctrinal decisions. Yet this dependence on the state was not resented by most churchmen, or at least not by the higher prelates. All the French bishops were nobles, accustomed to loyalty to the Bourbon monarchy. Beyond this, state control did not seem to weaken the essential prerogatives of the Church in matters of education and worship. Nor did it seriously threaten the wealth of the Church.

The Church did have great wealth. The lower clergy was typically ill paid, but wealth abounded for the Church as a whole and for the higher prelates. The economic power of the Church had two bases. First, there were substantial holdings in land. The Church may have possessed as much as one-tenth of the total lands of France. Second, there was independent taxing power over most citizens, through the tithe. Theoretically the tithe was to represent a full tenth of all production. In practice it now drew, on the average, only one-thirtieth. But this was certainly sufficient to assure a solid financial base.

Outside of France many churches lacked such extensive powers. The Irish Church, though commanding the loyalty of most of the population, was poor and persecuted. The Church in Holland and in some German states had only a minority position. The international Church, however, did have significant political powers through alliances with monarchy and through landed holdings. Most important, the papacy relied on its political position. It directly controlled central Italy, in the Papal States; and it carefully sought to foster this control by suppressing agitation and refusing any freedom of political activity. The Papal States represented important revenues and political independence for the papacy.

Despite many regional variations, then, the Catholic Church had a vital stake in the established order in 1789. It had real economic power and generally had an important political role. It would naturally be inclined to resist any effort at major social change. At the same time, particularly in France, the powers of the Church and the traditional association with the monarchy made it inevitable that any attack on the political and social order would be an attack on the Church as well. A clash was unavoidable, although the revolution ultimately carried its attack further than it needed to and thereby incurred unnecessary Catholic hostility.

Enlightenment philosophy, which was fundamentally anti-Catholic, attacked the political powers of the Church as part of the general attack on legal inequalities. It denounced the wealth and corruption of the higher clergy and blasted the Church's efforts to restrain freedom of speech and expression. The Enlightenment denied two traditional bases of Catholicism by substituting the idea of a rational universe, operating on uniform scientific principles, for the idea of an active, intervening God, and by replacing faith by individual reason as the primary means of obtaining necessary knowledge, even in the religious sphere.

The Church recognized the Enlightenment as a threat, and several Catholics undertook a refutation of the doctrines. Their posture was essentially defensive, rejecting not only Enlightenment doctrines but also the scientific discoveries on which they were presumably based. Church schools and seminaries sedulously avoided discussion of the new scientific issues. Yet these efforts at defense were not fully successful and the new doctrines continued to spread, reaching only a small minority of the population at first but spreading steadily. Certainly their exponents outdid their Catholic rivals in dynamism and polish. Though Catholicism was losing its place in intellectual life, most churchmen seemed content to ignore the problem. And even those who did not lacked the vigor and breadth of knowledge of their opponents. Many in educated circles were convinced that Catholicism was unable to cope with modern intellectual trends.

Some elements of the French population had lost active religious feeling by 1789, in some cases because of exposure to Enlightenment ideas. The professional groups, though not on the whole anti-Catholic, were increasingly lukewarm in religious sentiment and behavior. More important, significant segments of the peasantry had probably lost interest in religion by this time. When and why this development occurred is largely unclear. And it is certainly true that the Church did not feel a need to recognize this problem until the revolution heightened it. Clear, widespread irreligion was an issue only in the nineteenth century. But the spread of increasing religious apathy was a contributory factor in the revolutionary attack on the Church.

The revolution, of course, ultimately undermined the

Church most of all, although few of the early revolutionaries had been anti-Catholic and many churchmen, particularly in the lower ranks, were sympathetic to the early revolution. Neither side won total victory in the upheaval that led to implacable hostility between the two forces, but the Church was clearly diminished by the conflict.

Several revolutionary principles inevitably touched the Church. The revolution proclaimed religious freedom early. The state would no longer enforce restrictions on the press or on teaching in the interests of the Church. The Church would now have to compete with Protestantism or irreligion on its own and on an equal footing. Here was a major change. In association with other aspects of the revolutionary attack, it brought the Church to explicit hostility toward the principle of liberty.

The revolution also proclaimed legal equality. No citizens or institutions would have special privileges under the state. This meant the end of special ecclesiastical courts, the end of Church exemption from taxation, the end of the tithing system. Tithes were abolished as part of the destruction of feudal dues, which wiped out half the revenue of the Church.

Finally, the early stages of the revolution saw a direct attack on the remaining economic base of the Church: the land. Partly because the revolutionary government needed funds, partly because of the widespread hostility to Church wealth and worldliness, the landed holdings of the Church were seized. By 1790 the Church had lost its political privileges and powers and its economic independence. Moreover, the upper clergy, attached to the principles of aristocracy and monarchy, were shocked by the early revolutionary acts. These early changes introduced by the revolution inevitably brought others—and Church opposition—in their wake.

After depriving the Church of its economic support, the revolution sought some new system of ecclesiastical finance and administration. Instead of cutting the Church loose from the state, the revolution sought to maintain an attachment, but in new ways. The revolutionary tradition in France urged religious liberty, but not separation of Church and state. The American response to this issue was never seriously considered; and that fact was to color French history for the next century. For some revolutionaries state involvement in religious affairs seemed logical as a boon to Catholicism—the Church might need reforming for the sake of religion itself. For others the Church seemed too powerful to be left alone; it had to be controlled. For many, increasingly, the state was seen to have positive duties in the religious sphere, to purify France from the evils of excessive religion. In all this the tradition of Church-state linkage played a vital role. It was almost impossible to envisage a separation.

The first act of new association was in the economic sphere. To compensate for the seizure of Church lands, the government undertook to pay the salaries of all churchmen. Now that they were paying for the Church, it seemed logical that the revolutionaries should reform it. The result was the Civil Constitution of the Clergy, passed in 1790. Under this, the revolutionaries tried to raise the conditions of the lower clergy and diminish the opulence of the prelates. They reduced the number of dioceses. Most important, they decreed that bishops should be elected by all citizens in the diocese. An obvious attempt to impose revolutionary principles on the Church itself, this law directly contradicted the Church tradition of firm hierarchy and of transmission of ecclesiastical office through divine ordinance. It was a measure the Church could not accept.

By 1792 the Church was virtually at war with the revolution. Papal condemnations rained on specific acts of the French government and on the whole movement. Half the French clergy refused even superficial loyalty to the revolution. Some went abroad. Others stayed home and worked in secret to maintain the faith. A few even led counterrevolutionary efforts, causing the revolutionaries to attack Catholicism itself as near treason. In the cities particularly, where commitment to the revolution was strongest, many elements of the population from this time forward were to equate religion with political reaction and to reject it on these grounds. The most radical phase of the revolution saw the Church outlawed and priests persecuted and often killed. There were efforts to set up rival, revolutionary religions. When the revolution began to invade other areas, it extended its attacks on the Church. Even the Papal States were invaded, driving the pope to helpless dependence on any governments that would oppose the revolution.

By the late 1790's, and certainly under Napoleon, part of the breach between Church and revolution was healed. The state of war could not last, for the regular conduct of the Church was impossible with state hostility and a stable state could not exist with active Catholic hostility.

Both sides were impelled to a truce, which came with the Concordat of 1801. This was the basic document of Church-state relations in France for the nineteenth century. The Church was proclaimed the religion of the majority of Frenchmen, though not the religion of state. It was to receive state pay. Persecution of Catholicism would end. With new strengthening of the hierarchy within France, the power of bishops was increased; they named the priests of their diocese and could even control their movements. For these gains, however, the Church surrendered a great deal. The abolition of Church lands and tithes was officially recognized. Religious liberty was accepted. The state appointed the archbishops and bishops, who could not meet without government approval. Papal communications with the Church required official authorization. The Church, then, was largely decentralized, incapable of presenting a united front to the government. Dependence on the government became greater than ever before. Pope Pius VII, in accepting the Concordat, did stabilize the political position of the Church in France. But the concessions he reluctantly granted revealed how much of the old-regime Church the revolution had destroyed.

The later stages of the revolutionary and Napoleonic periods brought new dangers for the Church. Partly because of the rift with Catholicism, the state now actively sought to take over many functions previously reserved to the Church. Record-keeping was now put under the state. The government developed some charity efforts, through local charity bureaus; and the Church, with its weakened financial position, could not compete easily in this area. Most important, the state moved to control education. There was talk of a secular system of primary schools, but little was done. Under Napoleon, however, the University was established. This was a state body with a monopoly on higher education, particularly the secondary schools. The government created an elaborate system of *lycées*, secular and even anti-Catholic in tone. Again, lacking the funds, the Church could not compete; furthermore, state authorization was required to establish any private secondary school. A traditional sphere of the utmost importance was being taken away.

The fact was that the Church, though now formally at peace with the achievement of the revolution, was dependent on an essentially a-religious state. Napoleon saw the need for some accommodation with the Church, but he had no interest in serving its goals. He continued to undermine religion in the schools, in police pressure on Catholics, and in his treatment of the pope. The Church had no independent base from which it could strike back. Its financial problems were aggravated by the niggardly Church budget of the Napoleonic state. The Church had no influence on state censorship, no privileges in courts of law. In this situation there could be no active loyalty to the Empire, but there was, equally, no chance for effective resistance. Having already tried, and failed in, resistance, the Church was now too weak, its personnel too few and too old, even to contemplate opposition.

The internal structure of the Church was severely damaged. Literally thousands of parishes were left without a priest by 1815, and little possibility existed for recruitment of new clergy. The regular clergy, responsible for so much of the charitable and educational work of the Church, had been almost entirely disbanded; among other things, the government no longer enforced the sanctity of religious vows. Many Church buildings had been badly harmed by riots during the revolution, and there was no money for repairs. Few seminaries could be operated, even under Napoleon, which increased the shortage of priests and retarded any modernization of seminary curricula despite the continuing challenge of new ideas. One of the unusual characteristics of Lamennais, as a priest during the early Restoration, was the breadth of his training and his exposure to the Enlightenment philosophies; this was due not to ordinary clerical training but to its absence.

Clearly these factors resulted in the further weakening of Catholicism in society. De-Christianization now became a recognized problem. A generation of Frenchmen, between 1789 and 1815, was reared without regular religious training and, often, without religious practice. They were taught to regard the Church as an agent of superstition and reaction. And many, particularly in the cities, had new interests in politics and economic life for which religion seemed largely irrelevant. Many peasants were separated from the Church by a fear that the Church would seek a return of its lands that had been sold. Even more were affected by the vacancies in rural parishes. By 1815 whole rural areas were largely de-Christianized. Many businessmen and professional people were at best indifferent to religion. Many urban artisans were hostile to the institutional Church and considered it reactionary, even if they were often still personally religious. Catholicism still played an important role in the lives of most Frenchmen. But there existed a sizable minority that was fully alienated, and many more that were indifferent. And some of the groups hostile to religion were among the most articulate and politically active in France.

It was obvious to any churchman in 1815 that something had to be done about the revolutionary forces in France. The relationship with the government was unsatisfactory. The Church needed a more sympathetic environment in which to do its work; it needed more funds, more educational outlets. Anti-Catholic ideas had to be countered. Some effort had to be made to reconvert the masses of people who had abandoned the Church. Without renewed vigor on several fronts, the French Church seemed doomed to virtual destruction.

A Catholic revival was needed not only for the Church but for French society as well. France was tired in 1815. It had undergone twenty-five years of violent upheaval and foreign wars. It had been rent by divisions not yet healed. It had made itself a pariah among the European nations. It had allowed bloody persecutions and murders on French soil. Clearly France needed to return to the harmony and order of its traditional religion. The revolution had taught the penalties of attacking the faith. Without religion only force could rule. Without religion there was no restraint on the passions of men. Devotion to France seemed to the churchmen and to many others to involve renewed devotion to religion.

The need for religious revival was generally felt in the Church itself. A few took up the cause with particular ardor. Lamennais was among the most prominent of these.

Lamennais was born in June 1782, just seven years before the beginning of the revolution that was to dominate his life and France thereafter. His father, a merchant in Brittany, was preoccupied with business concerns. Lamennais was a difficult child, willful and temperamental. He was often ill. His mother died when he was six, and after her death his upbringing was haphazard. He was at first unusually pious, delighting in setting up statues of the Virgin and praying to them. He had no other intellectual interests as a boy. He long resisted reading, learning finally to oblige his nurse, the only member of the household for whom he cared. Even then he refused the education his father tried to impose upon him. His training was finally taken in hand by an uncle, Robert de Saudrais, a well-educated man who finally resorted to locking Lamennais in the library. The library contained many pious works and also a shelf of the modern philosophers labeled "hell." The boy was intrigued and soon found his interest deeply roused. From modern philosophers he turned to the classics. But his mind remained unreceptive to discipline.

During the revolution the royalist Lamennais family hid some persecuted churchmen, and the secret Church services fired Lamennais' imagination. In 1796 he was taken to Paris, where he was amazed at the freedom and diversity of opinions. But there was no clear sign that the revolution had yet attracted or repelled him. At most, his conservative and religious background tended to encourage a vague hostility to the revolution.

But by 1800, influenced by his philosophical readings, Lamennais had lost most of his religious fervor and even argued with the priest who prepared him for first communion. His emotional life, too, was deeply disturbed. He could not find the affection he needed at home; and then, as later, a feeling of not being loved plunged him into deep melancholy. About this time he seems to have fallen in love with a local girl, and been rejected. He was an ardent and intense young man, but he was extraordinarily ugly and had no clear prospects besides. A great problem now was what Lamennais was going to do for a living. His father had asked him to enter the business, but he had no taste for it. He sensed that life was passing him by. He had no profession, no family, no love.

His brother, Jean, had recently completed his training for the priesthood. By no means the intellectual equal of his younger brother, he had some experience in the world, and he was a man of decisive action. He had an obvious solution to his brother's depression and uncertainty: reintroduce a firm religion and prepare him for the priesthood. Jean had never had any doubts about religion or his calling; there was no reason to think that the same course would not work for his brother. Thus began the slow process of Lamennais' turning toward the Church, aided at every step by intense and loving advice. From this time onward a love of God and religion was to give focus to his life. Lamennais often claimed that he lacked the feeling for religion that he sought, that his approach was too intellectual, but his devotion could be intense despite his recurrent self-doubt:

See, my God, that I never forget and that I approach you as the angels themselves approach, trembling with respect, with a heart filled with the realization of its unworthiness, penetrated with your mercies, and embraced by [your] inexhaustible, immense, eternal love.[1]*

The form of Lamennais' religion was to change, but not his desire to rely on God. Just as religion gave him a certainty to cling to in a time of personal confusion, so he consistently felt that religion could provide a sure foundation for all men.†

Lamennais' new religious ardor increased his longing to

---

* Superior numbers refer to Notes, beginning on page 197.
† See Appendix A, 1.

escape the business world, but it did not give him an unmistakable calling to the service of the Church. He considered the Church outdated in certain ways, and he shied away from the discipline the priesthood would impose. Lamennais left his father's business and went to live at La Chesnaie, the small family estate in Brittany, near Dinan, where Jean joined him to direct his reading and study. Jean also introduced him to older priests there and in Paris; some took a warm interest in Lamennais and helped guide him toward the priesthood. Both Jean and Félicité were concerned with the decline of religious fervor in France; both were appalled at Napoleon's despotism and his scornful treatment of the Church. They began to prepare a denunciation of the forces of irreligion, notably the philosophies of the eighteenth century. By 1807, and twenty-five years old, Lamennais was still without a career. He decided that an ecclesiastical calling was his only choice, the only profession appropriate to his intellectual interests and his religious feelings. So, with considerable reluctance, Lamennais began the steps toward priesthood.

Lamennais was tonsured in 1809. He vowed to stop writing, as a renunciation of pride, but this intention faltered, and soon he was assailed with new doubts about his future. He believed he loved people too much to subordinate himself fully to the will of God. Yet there still seemed to be no professional or emotional alternative to the priesthood. He was later to find a girl to love, but it was after he had become a priest, and it was too late. He continued to defend the Church against attack, writing a short but bitter criticism of Napoleon's divorce and attacking the Napoleonic school system, which impeded and closed many religious schools—including the one at which Lamennais was teaching. His new doubts were assuaged by other priests, who advised and guided him, convinced of his calling. Finally, in 1816, he yielded and entered the priesthood.

Lamennais' health deteriorated for several months after

his decision. He blamed his advisers for applying pressure. "I am and can henceforward be only extraordinarily unhappy,"[2] he wrote in a letter to Jean. Lamennais was to be an unusual priest in many ways. Never did he identify fully with the spirit of his profession, particularly with its discipline, and this was finally to lead him to a break with the Church. He was never especially responsive to the guidance of any bishop. He was excused from certain daily devotions because of his poor health, though he always prayed regularly. Except in public, he resisted the ecclesiastical costume, preferring to wear a straw hat and simple gray clothing. But priest he now was. He never had a parish, but he directed the spiritual lives of many friends and disciples, and he directed them with great care. If he never understood Church discipline, he did seek constantly to help the Church. A priest had a great spiritual mission, he believed, a mission toward the glorification of God and the guidance of men.

A man with a hunger for affection and approval, always responsive to kindness, his desire for friendship guided much of his life and dominated his correspondence. Lamennais, seldom at ease, sought often intense friendships to relieve his insecurity: "I have said it often and I feel it more each day; I am amazed that anyone can like me."[3] Throughout his association with the Church, he attempted to surround himself with young people, treating them with consideration and often affection. He was also a man who liked solitude. He almost never escaped a feeling of loneliness, and to some extent he reveled in it. Though he was often attracted by the excitement of Paris, he never really liked the city, and he seems to have been happiest at his Breton home, La Chesnaie. Other cities in which he stayed at key points of his career, notably Rome, never failed to annoy him. The decisive changes in his attitudes came during his visits to crowded cities, changes induced by exposure to urban vitality and the tension that it created in him.

Lamennais was always a moody person, capable of periods of great exaltation and fits of black depression. He was tormented by migraine headaches, toothaches, and frequent fainting spells. A chronic gastritis could incapacitate him for weeks at a time. In his worst seizures he surrendered to great rages and violent polemics. Life itself often seemed unbearable; on several occasions when he seemed near death, Lamennais professed to welcome this end to his suffering, but when he did not die, he returned to the life that held little pleasure for him increasingly convinced that he must have some special purpose for his existence.

Lamennais lived for his intellectual activity. Never adept at business matters, he often hovered near financial ruin but lacked the skill to do anything about it. He had no interest in sensual pleasures. He ate little and slept fitfully, and was up by five in the morning. Frequently he exhausted himself by his zeal for work. He wrote massively. His correspondence alone after 1816 fills several volumes; his published work fills many more. Almost always he had a major writing project in progress, and sometimes several. His interest in reading remained intense. He kept up with the principal productions in European philosophy and frequently tried to learn new languages to expand his range. He read widely in French literature and periodically delved into theology and history. Lamennais might go for weeks without seeing a newspaper, for in Brittany the important papers arrived late and unpredictably. But he could never be without them for long, and his thirst for current news steadily increased, and his personal letters, particularly after 1820, were filled with political comment.* His study and writing defined his life; aside from his friends and his God, he had no other interests. His was a life of the mind; as he wrote in 1817, "everything is derived from doctrines."[4] His mission had to be first and foremost an intellectual one.

By 1816 Lamennais was convinced that his society was in

* See Appendix A.

movement and disorder. He had grown up with the revolution; he accepted it as a fact, as did most of his contemporaries, in contrast to many older Frenchmen. He knew also that the revolution had brought political instability and several unacceptable regimes and was convinced that it was a despotic force. He had experienced the oppression of the Church, to some extent personally, under Napoleon. So great was his fear of tyranny, in fact, that he had fled to England when Napoleon briefly returned to power in 1815. Partly from his own experiences, then, and more from the environment in which he had grown up, Lamennais had a sense of the power and the danger of the revolutionary movement. Though his political views changed greatly, he never fully lost a sense of the irrevocability of aspects of the revolutionary changes and of the need for order, for protection against both anarchy and tyranny.

Lamennais saw as the root cause of the social ills of his time the division of ideas in France and particularly the corrosive effects of eighteenth-century philosophy. Never would he abandon the conviction that Enlightenment thinking was unsound, that in relying on individual reason it failed to provide a principle that would unite men's beliefs. Never would he abandon the idea that men's beliefs should be united for a truly orderly society; never, given his intellectual bent, would he cease to maintain that the state of men's minds was the basis of all else in society. Lamennais' first major writing effort was an attempt to deal directly with the problems of belief. But even later, as he apparently turned more directly to politics, he adhered to this fundamental sense of the need to change men's minds. He sought a political arrangement in which the effects of division of beliefs could most successfully be overcome, and through this he hoped to attain true political order and a lasting accommodation with the forces of revolution.

After 1817 Lamennais would often profess to give up his

whole effort, to let society go its own way. But he never could. Lamennais could never stand criticism, and there was always some new critic to attack. Always there was some new point to be made, based on his further study and his understanding of politics. And always there was his deep sense of intellectual purpose.

Here was a mission to give focus to Lamennais' life. Here was a way to express both his piety and his concern for the social state of France. Here was a way to give meaning to his priestly office. The restoration of the true Church in French society became Lamennais' overriding goal for the next twenty years.

CHAPTER III

LAMENNAIS AND THE CHURCH
IN THE RESTORATION

The years after 1815 seemed auspicious for a Catholic revival. The government was now sympathetic, for the Restoration monarchy saw the utility of an active and strong Church. In its basic principles the monarchy was opposed to some aspects of the revolution; here was an obvious motive for alliance with a Church that had similar interests. Even a skeptic such as Louis XVIII offered many favors to the Church; his brother, later Charles X, was to promise many more. Outside government, there were currents in the intellectual community favorable to the Church. Many writers were tired of revolutionary excesses and the revolutionary principles as subjects for debate. The Romantic movement, spreading now to France, encouraged attention to the French past, of which religion was part, and to the beauties of religion, however irrational. Chateaubriand had already written in praise of Catholicism. Younger Romantics, such as Lamartine and Hugo, were sympathetic in their early careers. Finally, some of the revolutionary passions seemed to have cooled. The ardent revolutionaries had to bear the blame for revolutionary excesses and, to an extent, for the final defeats of the Empire. France seemed in a mood for calm and for some reconsideration of her recent past. Surely religion could gain from this mood.

Lamennais, like most thoughtful churchmen, was conscious of the possibilities of the new period. He saw the opportunities for Catholic revival and became one of the symbols of that revival. And, as he proclaimed his devotion to the advancement of the Church, the clergy widely hailed his early efforts. However, Lamennais' approach to the rejuvenation of Catholicism differed in two crucial ways from the interests of most of the French Church.

First, Lamennais did not see the Church's political position as the primary problem. He hated the revolution and was actively concerned with basic political structure; but he did not regard an active concern with daily politics as the proper focus for the Church. Rather than fussing about the precise arrangements of Church-state relations, Catholics should attack the fundamental evil of the revolution: the intellectual chaos the revolutionary principles entailed. A concerted attack had to be mounted against these principles and a realistic set of alternative, Catholic principles offered. Most leading churchmen disagreed with this orientation. They were interested in resisting revolutionary ideas and on this basis had some early sympathy for Lamennais. But for them the main problem was political. The whole tradition of the French Church seemed to require a satisfactory working arrangement with the state. Now that the government was again headed by a Bourbon monarch, the Church could turn to the state in the traditional manner. Hence, though Lamennais, too, was initially sympathetic to the restoration of the monarchy, his focus differed from that of his Church.

The one political concern that Lamennais consistently manifested directly contradicted the interests of the French hierarchy. Lamennais was an ultramontane; and this belief in the supremacy of the pope in the Church constituted Lamennais' second point of divergence. This position was consistent with his primary interest in an intellectual change. He thought that it was neither necessary nor possible to build a satisfactory political system until men's minds had been cured of the revolutionary evil. The Church, having the answer to the intellectual chaos of France, should therefore concentrate on its own strength, independent of an inevitably disorderly state. The Church would be strongest if centrally organized, and the papacy represented precisely the principle of order needed in the Church and through the Church in society. Again, this interest ran counter to the concern of the French Church to strengthen its relations with the state. On these grounds, Lamennais encountered the hostility of most French prelates quite early; on the same grounds, he won great sympathy from the pope.

The fact was that the Restoration and its policies toward the Church were judged differently by different groups of Catholics, with most of the French hierarchy at one extreme and Lamennais at the other. There were both gains and losses to organized religion in the new relationship of Church and state. Most Catholics stressed the gains, but Lamennais increasingly saw only the losses. This brought him into ever more active involvement with politics and issues of Church-state relations and made the gap between him and the leaders of the French Church increasingly apparent to both sides. Lamennais was attacked with a growing frequency; this drew him into active debate with the hierarchy. And Lamennais saw that a purification of Church politics was essential if his own primary interests were to predominate. This gradual drawing together of Lamennais and politics led to his final crisis with the Church as a whole.

To the leaders of the French Church, the Restoration seemed to be the answer to all their problems. The new government promised respect and sympathy for Catholicism; in the Charter of 1815, in fact, Catholicism was proclaimed the religion of state. The old-regime relationship between Church and state was not restored, but harmony existed in most matters of mutual interest. The bulk of the French hierarchy was satisfied with the religious tone of the state. There was hope, moreover, that the state could provide active assistance in dealing with the other problems of the Church. State aid could facilitate the reconversion of the indifferent. Police and censorship power could restrain the attacks on religion. Even in facing the broad social and intellectual problems of the Church, the attachment to a friendly state seemed vital. Finally, most of the French hierarchy was sincerely devoted to the Restoration monarchy as the proper political system. Most bishops were aristocrats still. Even those named by Napoleon found attachment to legitimate monarchy quite natural; and new, legitimist bishops were named during the Restoration.

For the leaders of the Church, then, loyalty to the Bourbon monarchy involved more than expedience; there was emotional commitment as well. In both religion and politics, the monarchy seemed the only barrier to a return to chaos. To be sure, specific acts of the monarchy toward the Church caused complaint, and it was certainly recognized that the Church had not regained its old-regime position. But it was far better off than it had been for a quarter-century, and there was simply no alternative in these evil times. Many members of the hierarchy had suffered directly at the hands of the revolutionary government. Though the Church was still attacked by the heirs of the revolution, the state seemed to assure protection to the Church despite the attacks. The Restoration provided a haven for the Church that could not be scorned.

Outside the French hierarchy, loyalty to the Bourbon monarchy was less intense. The papacy, for example, saw grave drawbacks in the new government. The popes recog-

nized, like the French prelates, that the old regime was gone
forever; there was no use addressing complaints to the government on this score. But there was real resentment against
the government's effort to cut the Church off from papal
control in the interests of promoting the Gallican traditions
and state authority. A clash occurred quite early. The
papacy in 1816 opened negotiations with a view to making
certain changes in the 1801 Concordat. No total revision was
sought, but the pope did hope to increase the number of
dioceses in France and win a few other concessions. The
French government did not resist these demands, but did
insist that the Gallican liberties of the French Church,
against Rome, be endorsed. This the pope would not grant.
Renewed negotiations in 1817 led to an agreement on increasing the number of dioceses. But the pope, Pius VII,
proclaimed this agreement as arising from his full authority.
This aroused Gallican hatred of papal control, and the government soon withdrew the whole project. It was apparent
quite early, then, that the intentions of the monarchy and
those of the pope differed. Though both sought to further
the Church, each attempted to increase its own control in
the process. The interests of the papacy and of the French
bishops also differed in this matter. The bishops, imbued
with the Gallican tradition, sought to please the state by
their loyalty. They tended to see the monarchy as a more
effective recourse than the papacy. These tensions between
Rome and the French government and hierarchy affected
most of the activities within the French Church in the period; they were vital to Lamennais' career.

Despite divergence of interests, the pope supported the
Restoration monarchy against any possible attack. For the
pope, too, there was no alternative. Rome recognized that
the Restoration offered more to the Church than would any
other conceivable regime. Rome, like the French bishops,
was committed to the principle of legitimacy. The political
outlook of the papacy was formed above all with an eye to

the safety of the Papal States, which the revolution had attacked. The Hapsburg monarchy, now firmly installed in
northern Italy, served as a guarantor to the restored Papal
States; and the Hapsburg ministers urged legitimacy above
all else. Both for the whole Church and for the French
Church, support of legitimate monarchs seemed the only
course. At times, as in 1828, the papacy even cut off the rare
protests of French bishops against government acts, urging
unconditional loyalty and obedience. And in general papacy
and hierarchy were united in their desire for an alliance of
Church and monarchy.

Within the French Church there was only one element
that did not fully share the sense of commitment to the Restoration government: the growing numbers of young priests.
There was, though, little outright disagreement; at most
there was a vague sense of unease. The Church now drew
tens of thousands of young men into the priesthood. This
was part of the revival of the Church under the Restoration.
Most of these new priests were conservative; many came
from legitimist families. Yet they did not think in precisely
the same terms as did their older colleagues or the hierarchy. Having grown up in the revolutionary period, they
had been touched by it. Though they hated it, they sensed
its reality in a way that most older churchmen never could.
The new priests could be less satisfied simply by a return to
association with a friendlier, more traditional state. Though
they were commonly legitimists, their legitimism lacked the
emotional fervor possible to men reared in the old regime.
Finally, the young priests often worked most directly with
the French people. They saw the widespread indifference.
They faced attacks phrased in Enlightenment terms. They
felt that something should be done. Again, the political position of the Church seemed less transcendently important
than it did to the older prelates. The gap in generations in
the French clergy had real significance.

Nevertheless, this gap could not easily result in a clear

difference of views on the Restoration government. The young priests were legitimists, they did not seek alternative political forms. The bishops, whose power in the French Church was great, maintained the virtues of the established order. And the Restoration did bring clear benefits to the Church and to the younger clergy. Since the orientation of the young priests created an openness to some novelty, these men became the principal audience for the few conscious Catholic innovators, of whom Lamennais was the chief. But there was no clear modification of the attachment of the French Church to the restored monarchy.

In this situation, the overriding interest of the Church lay in creating a favorable relationship with the government, presumably the key to the solution of all other problems. Through the various contacts with the government, a number of real gains were made. The state provided legal recognition and public support for the Church. Ordinances required shops to close on Sunday. Divorce was outlawed. The famous Sacrilege Law, passed in 1825, provided the death penalty for desecration of a Catholic Church. The measure was never enforced, but it stood as an extreme case of the official backing given to the Church. This backing took less formal guise as well. Religious practice was made part of the life of the royal court. An extreme instance was Charles X's consecration in the Cathedral of Rheims, which revived the old forms of accession to the throne through the grace of God and the Church. Public officials participated regularly in Church festivals and processions, which regained something of their old pomp and solemnity. Some churchmen served as political advisers and ministers of state; many bishops were named to the House of Peers. The union of Church and state was clear.

To an extent, there was more form than substance to this union. Catholicism was the religion of state, but Protestantism and Judaism were tolerated, and received financial support from the government. Churchmen served in various government positions, but in few cases was their authority great. State censorship purported to protect religion, yet anticlerical tracts were published without difficulty. Although some prelates undoubtedly hoped for a full return to the old-regime relationship of Church and state, none resulted. Yet the public recognition was welcome, and particularly under Charles X the devotion of the monarch to the cause of religion was clear and open.

There were two vital areas, furthermore, in which substantive advances were made. A partial union was effected between the Church and the state education system. The University structure was not dismantled and higher education remained largely a state monopoly. But two changes were made. First, the government authorized a significant number of Church secondary schools, both for the training of priests and for the education of Catholic laymen. Restrictions were imposed on the schools for laymen in 1828, but the Church could still maintain a limited secondary system. The University itself was placed in the hands of churchmen, for the two ministers of education during the Restoration were Church prelates. The state named Catholic almoners for the secondary schools, so that students would not be deprived of religious guidance. Twenty of the twenty-five rectors in the system were ecclesiastics, and three-quarters of the professors of philosophy in the secondary schools were clerics. In theory, at least, monthly confession was required of all students. The Church did not control the system, but exerted its influence in many vital areas.

More important still, state financial backing for the Church increased. By the end of the Restoration the ecclesiastical budget was more than double what it had been in the Empire. The Church was able to expand its primary schools. Teaching orders were reintroduced to serve in these schools and also in many schools established by Catholic laymen. The Church could take a growing role in education at all levels. Church buildings, often damaged and almost always badly maintained during the revolution and Empire, could now be restored or replaced. Most important, with more money for clerical salaries and for seminaries in which new priests could be trained, the Church could replenish its personnel. The results were startling: in 1815 nearly one-third of the parishes in France were vacant; many others were staffed by aged priests. By 1830 almost all the vacancies had been filled. In 1814, 715 men had been ordained priests. By 1821 the number was up to 1,400; in 1829, 2,350 priests were ordained. There was a total of 36,000 to 40,000 new priests. Enrollment in the larger seminaries had quadrupled. Scholarships could now be granted so that poverty did not bar the way to the priesthood.

There was more than direct state finance involved in all this, of course. Private gifts to the Church, encouraged by favorable state legislation allowing the Church to accept property, increased almost twentyfold. Certainly the atmosphere of public encouragement of religion played a great role. The Church became one of the clear channels to success and influence. Support for the Church was now a corollary of support for the monarchy and the established order. Yet the relationship to the state was the basis for the flowering of the Church. State favor, state offices, state finance, had raised the Church from near ruin. Almost every index showed progress. To prelates committed to the traditional association with legitimate monarchy in any case, there seemed no reason to question the merit of the present association. Most would have echoed the sentiments of the Bishop of Troyes when he affirmed "the eternal contract between throne and altar, neither of which can exist without the other."[1]

With this focus on politics, the questions of intellectual activity and of contacts with other segments of French society received inadequate attention. Even here, however, some gains were made. Published defenses of Catholicism increased substantially compared to the revolutionary period; Lamennais' efforts were long seen as part of this movement. Good-book societies sought to distribute religious pamphlets as widely as possible. Missions were established to spread Catholicism in the de-Christianized areas of France. Preaching a revivalist religion of an angry God and awful damnation, priests roused intense emotion in many rural areas. And the renewal of Church personnel alone helped expose larger numbers of Frenchmen to Catholicism than had been the case for over a generation. Grave weaknesses existed still in the social and intellectual position of the Church, but signs of revival did emerge.

Particularly encouraging were the new attitudes of many leading intellectuals and of the leading social class. Whereas the most prominent writers of the eighteenth century had been hostile to the principles of Catholicism, the new generation of intellectuals seemed favorably disposed. This was the period of early Romanticism in France. Such writers as Hugo and Lamartine were beginning their work. They were not really Catholic, for the most part, but they saw some of the beauties of religion. The young Lamartine was even moved to praise the consecration of Charles X at Rheims. These writers at least avoided attacks on the Church. This change of intellectual mood in France seemed to improve the standing of religion.

The same period saw the definite reconversion of the aristocracy to religion. In the eighteenth century many leading aristocrats had been attracted to the doctrines of rational skepticism. A few still maintained this position; Louis XVIII was probably one of them. But for the class as a whole, skepticism was now decidedly unfashionable. After all, the revolution had attacked aristocracy and religion simultaneously, and in the name of rational principles. Clearly, then, the two forces should be united for defense. But more than political expediency was involved. Many aristocrats had lived in exile; some had been imprisoned. For the class generally, religion seemed a vital solace in a period of unusual uncertainty, and a sincere piety prevailed in many leading families. This change, of great comfort to the French Church, brought a large increase in voluntary gifts. Much of the clergy thought of society in hierarchical terms, with the nobility at the top. If the leading class was devoted to the Church, the social position of the Church was satisfactory. The prelates themselves were largely aristocratic. The Archbishop of Paris even wrote a tract purporting to prove that Mary had been nobly born. It would have been difficult to deny that the Church had regained much of the ground it had lost in French society.

To the institutional French Church, the Restoration was bringing progress on virtually every front. There were, at the same time, vital weaknesses in the Church's position. These weaknesses could be seen during the period; Lamennais' career was devoted to pointing them out and, he hoped, to remedying them. The drawbacks in the Church's position, even the decline of Catholicism in this period, stand out still more clearly with the aid of hindsight, with the knowledge of the steady loss of adherents and the ultimate political defeat of the French Church. By almost any modern political standard, including that of contemporary Catholicism, it is hard to sympathize with the attitudes of leading churchmen in the Restoration—and it is easy to admire most features of Lamennais' liberal Catholicism. This orientation is unavoidable and is historically accurate in many ways. Two main points must be understood. First, Church policies in the Restoration were successful according to most reasonable standards of measurement. Progress was particularly clear on the institutional side, and this seemed most important. But even in other areas gains were being made. Second, the criteria used by Church leaders to judge their situation differed from those Lamennais employed. These men were dominated by their traditions and by the defensive mentality that the revolution had fostered. They felt that a strong monarchy was a good in its own right, that special attention to the aristocracy was normal. As the Restoration brought progress in the relationship of the Church to both bodies, it brought undeniable benefits for religion itself.

The Church established, then, a distinct political orientation. It sought intimate, mutually favorable contacts with the legitimate monarchy. It assumed or hoped that the revolutionary currents were past or could be repressed. It favored some new intellectual activity, but generally avoided a frontal attack on rationalist and scientific arguments, again on the assumption that these ideas could be safely ignored and repressed. Although aware of its need to deal with widespread loss of religious feeling, the Church focused on the upper groups in society more than on the lower, and relied primarily on strengthening its own personnel and institutional structure. And most of these policies seemed to be working.

There were drawbacks, however. The social and intellectual problems were glossed over more than they were met. The political policies of the Church heightened the difficulties in both spheres. There was even some trouble with the state.

Monarchists, like the churchmen, argued and believed that the union of throne and altar was essential. Although most of them were sincerely religious, they naturally tended to use the Church for their own purposes. This could involve sacrificing Church activities if the interests of state required. In 1828, under the pious Charles X, the Jesuit order was banned in France and Catholic secondary schools were severely restricted. The reason: liberal attack on the monarchy was increasing and some changes in religious policy

seemed the easiest way to appease it. The refusal to alter the
Concordat significantly was another sign of the divergence
between government and Church interests, for what the
government sought was full control over the Church. It assumed that this would not harm religion, but this was not
the main point. Church activities, especially those not firmly
under the control of the loyal hierarchy, were kept under
police watch. There was even some censorship of religious
writings. Lamennais, because he attacked the government's
religious policy, was brought to trial and fined. Contacts
between the French Church and the papacy were systematically discouraged. The government ordered adherence to the
Gallican ideas of state direction of the Church. These policies did not usually displease the French hierarchy, though
there were certainly many protests over the 1828 measures.
The hierarchy was sympathetic to Gallicanism and state
direction; and the state could perpetuate this attitude by
naming only Gallican bishops. Nevertheless, to those outside
the hierarchy the full identity of Church-state interests was
not clear. Too often the Church seemed a victim of reason of
state.

Furthermore, there were two areas in which the Church's
political policies were not fully successful; both related to
the broader problem of the social position of Catholicism.
Though the Church made major gains in education during
the period, it did not really control the upper schools. The
government allowed great Church influence and direction
by churchmen, but the secular tone of the schools often remained. Many teachers were deists. Much of the teaching
was non-Catholic or even anti-Catholic. Anticlerical pamphlets circulated in many schools. At the college of Sainte-
Barbe, students took a vote on the existence of God; God
won, but by only a single vote. It seems clear that only a
massive educational effort could have wiped away the
legacy of Enlightenment and revolution. But at the higher

levels, where the leaders of France were trained, the Church was prevented from making this effort. It could not run its own system. As a sop, it was given superficial control of the state system, but this was not enough. The essence of the system remained secular. Possibly the problem was insoluble; possibly nothing could have wiped away the earlier damage. But the Church was not given the chance that many Catholics felt it should have had. Among the people most bitter about this were many young almoners at the state schools. Several later joined Lamennais, and one, Jean Baptiste Henri Lacordaire, became a leader in the Mennaisian movement. Much of French liberal Catholicism was based on this real weakness in the Catholic position.

The second drawback of the Church-state link is more obvious. Anyone hostile to the monarchy or its policies would inevitably tend to be hostile to the Church as well. The two seemed inseparable, and both proclaimed their unity as a glory of the Restoration. Attacks on the government increased fairly steadily after 1825. At first the revolutionary mood seemed to have disappeared, for France was weary of dispute and war. The early Restoration government was careful to make many concessions to liberal principles. The revolutionary law codes and land settlements were retained. There was a parliament; freedom of the press was substantial; the Church was not restored to its old position. But liberal opposition to the government gradually swelled. The parliament did not have enough power and was too narrowly based. The government interfered with liberal University teachers and with the liberal press. The Church had undue political influence. With its revolutionary heritage, the liberal movement was naturally hostile to Catholicism. The link between the Church and an unacceptable state increased this hostility. The result was a widespread feeling that Church and monarchy had to be attacked together. Vivid, if largely untrue, rumors circulated about the secret power of Jesuits and other ecclesiastics in the government. Many religious policies of the government were regularly assailed.

The political stance of the Church was implicitly predicated on the notion that the forces of revolution could be kept down. This made good sense, since the revolutionaries had attacked the Church so bitterly before. But by the late 1820's the logic of this attitude could certainly be questioned. Most of the press was liberal, therefore bitter in its denunciations of the Church. The bulk of parliament was liberal. The whole movement threatened to win control, and the government seemed powerless to stop it. Still the Church seemed to ignore the danger and to cling ever more tightly to the beleaguered monarchy.

The concentration of the French Church on its political relationships had other disadvantages. First, though there were some improvements in seminary curricula, the education of priests was considerably behind the times. Scientific discoveries were ignored, as was Biblical criticism. There were no courses on Church history. Most of the training was still directed to older theological problems, such as the debate with the Jansenists about the importance of grace to salvation. There was little possibility, then, for ecclesiastics to come to grips with more modern intellectual problems. The vague, largely aesthetic, religious interest of the Romantics was no substitute for intellectual vigor in the Church itself, for the intellectual attacks on the Church did continue, largely in the spirit of the Enlightenment. The greatest French philosopher of the period, Victor Cousin, was anti-Catholic. Newspapers and schoolteachers both repeated Enlightenment arguments about the Church. By the later Restoration the reprinting of eighteenth-century rationalist tracts was one of the most popular publishing ventures in France. Against all this the Church had little to offer. A few individuals, Lamennais most notably, tried to meet the attack, but the Church as a whole lagged.

Finally, the Church was not really gaining ground in French society. The missions, the new aristocratic piety, the sympathy of some leading Romantics—all this might conceal the problem, but could not solve it. Large segments of the middle class were still hostile or indifferent. From this group, for example, came most of the young skeptics in the secondary schools. The de-Christianized rural areas had not returned to the fold. And there was a new problem, though still dimly perceived. The cities of France were growing. New commercial opportunities and the beginnings of factory industry drew thousands of people into old cities, such as Paris and Lyons, and new centers as well. The Church was ill prepared to deal with the newcomers. It did not establish physical facilities to handle the expanded urban lower class. Its clergy did not understand urban problems. The hierarchy was imbued with a distinctly preindustrial conservatism. The lower clergy was largely rural. The result was that a growing portion of the urban population was left untended by the Church. And this was at the time that city residents were acquiring increasing importance in society as a whole. There were hints already of the separation between the working class and the Church that would be obvious in later decades. Growing indifference in many cities added to the older difficulties of the Church among the peasants and the middle class.

In fact, religious feeling waned during the Restoration, despite all the improvements in the Church's position. There may have been an early wave of enthusiasm for religion, as part of the revulsion against the previous period of chaos; but this wave soon subsided. There were reports in 1829 that the number of Easter communions had dropped to one-third of the 1820 level. Church services generally were ill attended. The bulk of the population was still nominally Catholic, but for many this was truly in name only; and there was a growing minority that did not even bother with the name.

There was certainly ample basis for dissatisfaction among churchmen. This dissatisfaction was particularly acute among the younger priests. These were people who lacked the defensive sense born of direct experience of the revolutionary hardships. They could not be content with the institutional gains of the Restoration. They were often fired with a zeal for religion that they could despairingly contrast with the spirit of society generally. These were the people who encountered indifference most directly, in re-established parishes or in schools. These were the men who had first-hand knowledge of the intellectual attacks on the Church. The young priests were not alone. A number of Catholic laymen, generally young also, shared their concern for the place of religion. There was no formal movement of protest during the Restoration, nor was there ever to be. But there was a widespread feeling of unease. Lamennais was to share this feeling and to seek to guide it, though he only partially succeeded. He did not stand alone. But he was the most articulate and most radical of the many Catholics who perceived, at least vaguely, that the Church was on the wrong course.

Lamennais was early aware of the need for a rejuvenation of religion and early emerged as a leader of those who sought to grapple with the basic problems of the Church in modern times. He saw that the Church could not save itself without taking the offensive and that society was lost if the Church declined. Here was a cause to command complete devotion, which was to give focus to Lamennais' life for the next fifteen years. In 1817 Lamennais published the first volume of his *Essai sur l'Indifférence en Matière de Religion*. This book directly attacked what Lamennais felt to be the key evil of modern society, the reason for the decay of the social order and the related hostility to Catholicism: the belief in the primacy of individual reason, leading to irreligion and indifference to religion. The first volume dealt with the skeptical philosophies themselves, the heritage of the eighteenth century. Lamennais bent all his efforts to show the inadequacy of individual reason. His work proved extremely popular, for he was talking about topics of widespread concern. Thirteen thousand copies of his book were sold during the first year. Soon translations were made into the major European languages. Lamennais' reputation was quickly established. Later volumes of the *Essai,* which tried to construct an alternative to individual reason, were less popular, but the impression of Lamennais as an intellectual leader of the Church was not erased. The new priest was a symbol of the desire of many Catholics to fight back, to recognize their altered situation and deal with it realistically.

Despite his popularity, Lamennais did not have the interests and outlook of most of his audience. He could and did talk in their terms, but the roots of his concern were different. Lamennais was preoccupied with the problem of irreligion because of his deep-seated fear of social chaos. Throughout his career, he felt that religion was socially necessary: "without religion, no society."[2] Correspondingly, Lamennais worked sincerely for the good of religion; but this was less for religion's own sake than for its vital social role.

Partly because of the political experiences of his earlier years, Lamennais was convinced that men, by themselves, could not create a harmonious social order, for men were created equal among themselves, and among equals there could be no social rights and duties, no reason to obey. In other words, government was impossible, for it had no right to command its subjects. Society, then, had to rest on God. By establishing a system of eternal rewards and punishments, God had provided man with the only possible motive for sacrificing part of his natural equality to the interests of social order and unity. Since God had revealed His system to man by means of religion, religion was the foundation of society. It alone put order into society, by giving the reason for government and duties, by perfecting the laws, by purifying customs, by uniting all members of the social body in bonds of love. Even in the first volume of the *Essai* some of the bases of Lamennais' views were clear. Society had a vital need for unity, and religion filled this need. It gave the motive for obedience; it provided a shared belief that itself promoted harmony. And it guaranteed true liberty. For just as religion taught the masses that obedience to their rulers was obedience to God, so it protected them by showing the rulers the divine limits of their authority. Without religion, force alone could rule. From this standpoint, too, religion was a social necessity.

Lamennais believed in religion as the agency of salvation, but religion for its own sake in this sense did not greatly interest him. Furthermore, Lammenais was distinguished by his desperate fears both for society and for religion. As early as 1818, he began to predict horrors worse than those of the revolution.* This was to become a constant theme; dire prophecies of upheaval, of anarchy or despotism or both, were to fill Lamennais' mind from this time forward. His interpretation of the imminent upheaval did change with time, but not the prediction itself. Lamennais was convinced that the revolution was not over. Its causes still simmered in society. Any person or institution who did not bend every effort to deal with the revolutionary forces was blind and stupid. It was ridiculous to be complacent or content. Great changes were inevitable. To meet them, existing institutions and policies had to change. Lamennais was never convinced that the immediate prerevolutionary past could be restored.

* See Appendix B, 1.

At first he did look to the past, but to a more remote past; later he would abandon even this. Always he believed in the newness of the European situation and the need for radical measures to cope with it.

In 1817 the cause of the imminent social catastrophe was the philosophy of individual reason as the final judge of truth and certitude. The social dangers of this philosophy seemed obvious. Instead of accepting true religion and the divine obligation of obedience, men were submitting social structures to their individual judgments and often, with human conceit, rejecting them. As the only sanction for social order was being destroyed, the remedy seemed clear: Catholicism had to regain its hold, for it alone denied individual reason and insisted on obedience to higher authority.

It was easy to criticize individual reason and show its threat to society. Lamennais offered the criticism vigorously. He showed that reason cannot even prove its own existence. Without some instinct or faith, therefore, men can have no sure beliefs at all. Here was a frontal attack on the philosophy of Descartes, in many ways the basis of French rationalism from the seventeenth century onward. It was an attack that won wide respect.

However, Lamennais never sought to tear down; always he desired a constructive alternative. The bulk of his *Essai* was devoted to building a system to replace individual reason. His distinctive orientation became apparent. Lamennais did not simply urge faith in the Bible and Church authority. He tried to find a wider faith first. Lamennais, dominated by his sense of novelty, knew the old arguments, by themselves, would not work. Because so many men believed in their own reason, they could not be persuaded easily to accept faith. They had to be offered some criteria for belief that they could grasp in their own terms. Beyond this, Lamennais was a system-builder. Not content to echo older arguments, he tried to erect his own. The philosophy he did develop, the system of general reason, was not widely popular; in many ways it seems silly. But it is worth noting for two reasons. First, it showed Lamennais' desire to seek a basis for certitude independent of the Church itself, capable of appealing to men reluctant to accept the Church. Second, Lamennais himself continued to believe in his philosophy of general reason as his political views changed; ultimately he turned to it as an alternative to the Church.

According to Lamennais, truth could be found only by accepting what all men had believed at all times; this is what general reason was. General reason was infallible because it was founded on a revelation from God to man at the time of creation. This original revelation had included such truths as the existence of God and of eternal rewards and punishments—the same truths on which the possibility of society depended. Acceptance of general reason led necessarily to acceptance of the authority of the Church, since Christ came as a fulfillment of the truths in which men had always believed through general reason. Here was Lamennais' defense of Catholicism. It was an unorthodox one. Truth came from God, to be sure, but not originally through the Church. Although they would lead to the Church, the basic truths had been present in the human race long before the creation of the Church. But even now, one could presumably find truth by investigating human history. This is what Lamennais urged nonbelievers to do, for once general reason was accepted, men would abandon their corrosive individual judgment and would submit to higher authority.

There were churchmen, primarily Jesuits, who from the first criticized Lamennais' approach. Most bishops were also dubious, and the Mennaisian philosophy was not accepted in most seminaries. However, Rome refrained from criticism, if also from praise. Lamennais' popularity among many educated French Catholics was great. The Church had long tolerated a variety of Catholic philosophies, and Lamennais' intentions were clearly good. He had provided inestimable services, having brilliantly attacked religious skepticism. He had helped correct the impression of intellectual stagnation in the Church and was long to be a symbol of the intellectual vigor of Catholicism. His enemies were to plague and disgust him constantly, but he also had many defenders and a great reputation. He could be content with his work, but it was not in Lamennais' nature to be so. He had to defend his philosophy against its many critics. By the early 1820's his fame drew young disciples who had to be guided and used. The most important of the early converts was the abbé Gerbet, who was to be one of Lamennais' principal exponents until 1834. Finally, there were political problems to be treated. The *Essai,* not explicitly a political work, was designed above all else to solve fundamental social ills. It was the *Essai,* however, that drew Lamennais into politics. His desire to regenerate society, his view that the revolution was actively working still, had obvious political implications. The fame of the *Essai* attracted many requests from conservative politicians and newspapers for Lamennais' support, for it was assumed that a defender of religion was automatically a defender of monarchy and the whole established order. Lamennais was urged to bend his talents to political writing, and he could not resist. Religion needed a political as well as an intellectual defense. The ultimate hope for mankind remained the conversion of everyone to Catholicism, through the philosophy of general reason. In the meantime there was practical work to be done against the forces of irreligion and disorder, and Lamennais could never resist the excitement of politics and especially of political journalism. Although he did not abandon an interest in Catholic apologetics, from 1820 onward the attraction of politics became increasingly pronounced.

Lamennais seemed at first to be a Catholic monarchist, like most of the clergy of his day. He wrote in royalist newspapers because they alone would solicit work from a Catholic writer; this added to the impression of his being a monarchist. Lamennais did at first have some interest in the Restoration monarchy. He hoped the king would lead in repressing the revolution and guiding society back to Catholicism. However, Lamennais never felt an emotional loyalty to the monarchy. Always conceiving of the interests of the Church as separate from those of the government, he judged the government by its utility to the Church. Lamennais, convinced of the evils of the revolutionary political tradition, believed that democracy was diametrically opposed to religion, which preached supreme and unvarying authority. Although he did see the monarchy as embodying the principle of God's sovereignty, it was God's sovereignty that was important above all else.

By 1822 or 1823 Lamennais had abandoned the Restoration monarchy, incensed by the government's compromises with revolutionary and liberal forces. He was outraged by the state's toleration of Protestants and Jews—a clear sign that the monarchy was not supporting the true, religious basis of society. He was convinced that the monarchy was doomed, for instead of destroying the agents of anarchy, it compromised with them. As early as 1820 he wrote: "No one can sustain a government which abandons itself; no one can save it when it wishes to be lost."[3] Soon Lamennais decided that the state had become politically atheist and had officially abandoned all distinction between good and evil. Lamennais' orthodox political conservatism, always superficial, ended.

The destruction of the Restoration monarchy, which Lamennais began to predict at least by 1825, need not be a tragedy, he thought. It need not touch the true basis of political order, for the Church was the real guarantor of society.

A strong Church could "bring everything to unity, coordinate the nations as members of a single family in a system of universal fraternity, by obedience to their common Father, and establish the pre-eminence of rights over selfish interests by substituting justice for force everywhere."[4] As Lamennais had already implied, the basic social need for order and higher authority could be fulfilled only by the Church. As long as both people and rulers submitted to the higher jurisdiction of the Church, it really did not matter what political forms prevailed. By the middle of the 1820's, then, Lamennais devoted his attention to the preservation and promotion of the Church, independent of the monarchy. He stopped writing in newspapers, since the royalists, quite rightly, would not have him. But in various essays and in his letters, his concentration on the cause was clear.

To preserve both Church and society, it was of overwhelming importance to establish the authority of the papacy. This meant not only freedom from the interference of states but also the restoration of internal Church unity by the recognition of papal infallibility. Any Gallican attempt to restrain the pope by councils or other means was an act against the Church as Christ had created it. Furthermore, the powers of the pope over society had to be restored. God had erected the Church as interpreter and administrator of His divine laws; the pope was both the embodiment and executor of the social unity that God intended; the pope alone could restrain people from chaos and governments from despotism. Even if governments fell, the people would ultimately have to turn to the pope as the only means of founding a viable society. Sooner or later the pope would be called upon to regenerate humanity, both temporally and spiritually. As Lamennais wrote in 1825: "The future of the world is in his hands; . . . let him know it and let him fulfill his high destinies with confidence."[5]

Lamennais was one of the first and more vigorous ultra-

montanes in France. For the French Church, the idea of
papal supremacy was new, in modern times. The pope had
never been denied, but his powers over the French Church
had been indirect. For Lamennais, however, ultramontanism
was a vital doctrine. He was constantly seeking unity and
order. If there was no final authority in the Church, the
Church could not provide final authority for society. Moreover, the pope seemed the only alternative to a government
that Lamennais increasingly felt was useless. The state was
not really protecting the Church, so the Church, through
firm papal authority, had to defend itself. In this view, as in
many others, Lamennais anticipated a more general movement of Catholicism; more and more Catholics were to realize that the traditional reliance on government had to be
modified. In the 1820's ultramontanism was a radical view.
Lamennais encountered the bitter hostility of French bishops and of lay Catholics who sought to use the Church to
defend the monarchy. This opposition strengthened Lamennais' reliance on the pope; support from Rome was his only
recourse against attacks in France. The papacy would certainly support the ultramontane position, and friendly relations with Pope Leo XII confirmed Lamennais' loyalty. Finally, a growing number of younger Catholics, disappointed
with the government's treatment of the Church, began to
turn toward ultramontanism. They might not have shared
Lamennais' larger views on the pope as arbiter of society
generally, but they did approve of his desire for strong, central organization in the Church.

Defense of papal power and of the Church separate from
the state involved Lamennais in comments on current
Church-state relations. The monarchy, after all, was bent on
restricting papal influence in the French Church, and it
pressed the Gallican principles and appointed Gallican
prelates. On these grounds alone, Lamennais was impelled
to attack state control of the Church. He believed that the

state, while unjustly restraining the Church at every turn, at the same time was allowing anti-Catholic errors to go unchecked. Lamennais noted the restrictions placed on religious orders, though he himself felt that many of the orders were out of date. His main attack was on government limitations of Catholic education. The chief task for the Church, after all, was to spread Catholic doctrines to all men; if it could not do this freely, the whole structure of society was threatened. State control had come to be tyranny over the Church.

The alternative to this damaging association with the state was a system of liberty. Lamennais first considered liberty the best of possible evils. He had never advocated unrestrained state control; always divine laws were to limit government. But he had been long convinced that religious liberty could not be part of a proper political order, since there was only one religious truth. Denial of this truth should not be open to individuals, lest they lose their chance for salvation and destroy the only valid basis for society. However, Lamennais did recognize the need for liberty in the present sorry state of France. As early as 1819 he wrote in support of liberty of the press. Although liberty of the press was an evil, its existence was necessary for the free battle of ideas, in which truth would ultimately win. He applied the same reasoning to education. Ideally the state should support a Catholic system, but as it was not doing so, it was important to destroy the state monopoly and give Catholics a chance to spread their views in free competition. In other words, Catholicism needed freedom from a hostile government. It could neither demand nor receive its own freedom without accepting freedom for others. Lamennais wrote in 1818:

Who has more interest in demanding [religious] liberty than the Catholics? If it existed for them as it exists for the Protestants, for the Jews . . . their clergy would not experience continual

limitations in the exercise of their functions, they would not
every day be tormented by the administration.[6]

By 1825 Lamennais was halfway toward holding a liberal
Catholic view. He urged dissociation of Church and state.
Although he saw the practical need for complete religious
and intellectual freedom, he had yet to welcome liberty and
liberals. His desire for ultimate unity of belief blocked a
view of liberty as anything more than a temporary expedi-
ent. His hatred of revolutionary chaos, his recognition that
most liberals were hostile to religion, prevented any desire
for union with doctrinal liberalism. Lamennais' political
views were tinged with unusual pessimism in mid-decade.*
Obviously enjoying such forebodings, as always, he predicted upheaval and disaster. What would emerge was not
clear. There was a firm hope that ultimately men would turn
to the healing unity of the Church and the papacy. In the
meantime little could be done. The hierarchy was bent on
union with the state. The state was increasingly repressive of
true religion. Lamennais had to urge the Church to turn to
liberal expedients he distrusted. Since the main exponents of
liberalism were hostile to Catholicism, the immediate future
seemed ominous.

The middle of the decade was a period of transition for
Lamennais. The crest of enthusiasm for the *Essai* had
passed. Increasing criticism was developing over Lamennais'
ultramontanism, the concept of general reason, and his general independence from the French Church. Lamennais still
saw order in society, authority in the Church, and a massive
campaign to reconquer men's minds as the vital goals. But
he had not entirely formulated the means.

Certain bases, though, were being laid for later activity.
Most notably, a Mennaisian movement was under way, led
by young disciples who shared Lamennais' belief in universal

* See Appendix A, 2–5.

reason and in ultramontanism. In 1823 Gerbet and others founded the *Mémorial Catholique,* a monthly journal under Lamennais' unofficial guidance. For the remainder of the Restoration the *Mémorial* served as an organ for the Mennaisian school, attacking Gallicanism, defending the liberties of the Church, supporting Lamennais' philosophy against its many opponents, and trying to reconcile Church thinking with modern ideas. In 1824 Lamennais developed a plan to found a center for Catholic studies in all branches of knowledge. He believed a Catholic encyclopedia was needed, to combat the deist encyclopedia of the previous century. Early in 1825 Gerbet accompanied Lamennais to La Chesnaie, to found a center for the propagation of the Catholic idea in France. A few new recruits were enlisted, but funds were lacking, and there was only limited enthusiasm for the effort. Finally, Lamennais did not abandon his own writing efforts. He published the third and fourth volumes of the *Essai,* elaborating his view of the content of general reason. In 1825 he published *De la religion considérée dans ses rapports avec l'ordre politique et civil (On Religion Considered in Its Relationship with the Civil and Political Order).* In the book Lamennais asserted the atheism of the state and the need for religious liberty and papal authority. The book was not a great success. Liberals scoffed at the presumed insincerity of a Catholic liberalism. Most bishops objected to the book. Then, in 1826, the government brought Lamennais to trial for his views. The Mennaisian movement seemed to be at a low ebb.

Lamennais fell ill the next year. For some days he lay near death, wanting to die. He was exhausted from studying and writing and saw no clear support for his views. He had not been able to reach the public in any broad sense; yet his desire to convert men to Catholicism and his belief in general reason called for such contact with the people. The French Church was hostile to him, though Lamennais could explain this by claiming that the bishops were creatures of the government. More important was the silence of Rome, for Lamennais relied, both intellectually and politically, on papal support.

Lamennais did not die and he did not remain in a despondent mood. His sense of mission was perhaps increased by his recovery from illness: "I must employ for the defense of the Church the time which God perhaps left me only for this purpose."[7]

The year 1827 marks a turning point in Lamennais' career. The Mennaisian movement began to gain momentum. New recruits were drawn in, new organizations established. Lamennais' writing patterns began to change. He stopped writing lengthy treatises, with one exception, and began work on pamphlets and newspaper articles. He was trying to comment with immediacy and vigor on the issues of the day, and he was attempting to reach a broad audience. Most important, Lamennais' political views were changing. His basic interests remained—in the Church and papacy, in the fear of social chaos, in the hostility to the existing state. Elements of the earlier tone persisted, primarily in the predictions of imminent disaster. On balance, however, the position had changed. A tentative use of liberalism now became an eager espousal of liberal Catholicism. Uncertainty about the political future gave way to hope that a constructive movement could be established as soon as the present regime collapsed. The increase in Mennaisian activity and organization reflected the new decisiveness of Lamennais' views, with the growing dynamism of the movement reinforcing Lamennais' desire to guide the formation of a new social order.

His interest in liberty was not new. Even in the Empire Lamennais' hatred of tyranny had been clear. He had long urged greater liberty for the Church and had recognized that liberty for other groups was inevitable. However, always before there had been a fear of liberty and liberalism as a heritage of the revolution; always there had been the sensed incompatibility between freedom for the individual and the unity of belief on which orderly society was based. Now Lamennais accepted the revolution as a good thing, not in its entirety but in its fundamental intent. Now he saw a hope for an alliance between religion, the principle of order, and liberty, the principle of the revolution.*

In essence, Lamennais turned his long-held view that the forces of revolution were still at work into the basis for his new orientation. More than a decade had passed since the revolution had ended. Yet the revolutionary interests in liberty and political change had grown steadily stronger; it seemed clear to Lamennais that they would win out. If the Church maintained its attachment to the doomed monarchy, it too would be attacked. From a purely practical standpoint, the Church needed to come to terms with liberalism. Further, liberalism without the Church would be dangerous, for there was no acceptable substitute for Catholicism as a vital social force against anarchy. For Church, for society, for liberalism itself, a union of forces was essential. Beyond this, Lamennais saw the rising strength of liberalism as a sign from God; no movement could continue against His will. Lamennais had never been totally committed to the old regime; he had always written of the need for change and rejuvenation. Now, however, he began to speak of the possibility of a new social order, based on the permanent alliance between Church and revolution. Here was a glorious opportunity for a radically improved society.

Lamennais' liberal Catholicism seems, then, to have derived from a change in attitude toward the power and potential of liberalism. There was, however, more to it than that. Liberalism itself seemed to be changing. Most liberals remained anticlericals and were still hostile to the idea of re-

* See Appendix A, 6–9.

leasing the Church from state control. But there were younger liberals, organized around the *Globe* newspaper, who preached a reconciliation of the Church and the revolution. These men were not Catholics, but they saw no need for constant battle. Of all liberal papers, only the *Globe* defended Lamennais' position at the 1826 trial. Even in France, then, the idea of a liberal-Catholic union did not seem totally unrealistic.

In Belgium, at the end of the 1820's, such a union was actually taking place. Catholics were chafing under the restrictions of the Protestant king of Holland. Seminaries were regulated and sometimes closed, Catholics were denied government jobs, Catholicism in general was treated as dangerous and inferior. Belgian liberals had their own grievances against the Dutch king. They wanted Belgian independence on nationalist grounds; they sought freedom from Dutch-imposed economic restrictions. A common enemy served to unite Catholic and liberal leaders, even though Belgian liberalism itself had an anticlerical tradition. Lamennais' work was extremely popular there. His views on the Church's need for liberty explained and promoted Belgian liberal Catholicism. A leading Belgian Catholic wrote to a friend in 1826 about *De la religion considérée:*

If you haven't read abbé Lamennais' book, read it! If you have read it, read it again! If you have read it and reread it, make it the subject of your meditations! Learn it by heart. This is what I shall say to every sensible man.[10]

The Belgian developments confirmed Lamennais' sense that he was on the right path and impelled him to seek similar gains in France.

Lamennais remained ultramontane.* For a liberal Catholic, urging separation of Church and state, papal leadership seemed vital. Lamennais continued to believe in his basic

* See Appendix A, *10.*

view of the papacy, that the pope would ultimately provide the essential guidance to all men in the new society. But the pope, erring at the present time, countermanded the resistance of the French bishops to the ordinances of 1828, which limited Catholic seminaries. As the papacy did not actively support its ultramontane defenders, its silence was construed as support of the Gallicans. The pope was obviously allied with conservative powers to preserve the Papal States in Italy. Consequently, and in the short run, a movement had to be developed independent of, though not hostile to, the papacy that could carry on the essential union of Church and liberty until the papacy was ready to assume direction. Without this, society might disintegrate because of the temporary confusion of Rome.

For several reasons, then, Lamennais accepted the principles of liberalism and sought to build a liberal Catholic movement. He was not the only liberal Catholic leader, nor was he the first in France. But, because of his past reputation, he was the most prominent. A liberal Catholic paper had been founded in the mid-twenties by the Baron d'Eckstein, a converted Danish Jew; this was several years before Lamennais clearly espoused the movement. But the obscure baron, hampered by a turgid style, could not match the scintillating efforts of this established leader of Catholic thought. Lamennais gave liberal Catholicism a vitality and popularity its earliest leaders could not provide and easily became the guide for the movement in France.

In addition to leadership, Lamennais gave liberal Catholicism a dogmatism, a sweeping quality it might not otherwise have developed. As always, Lamennais systematized his thought; and he would not tolerate deviations. A liberal Catholic movement, largely independent of the Mennaisians, developed in 1829; it founded the newspaper *Le Correspondant*. This group urged freedom of Church and state and proposed a working alliance with sympathetic liberals. But it recognized some of the merits of the present system, sought to avoid shocking the sensibilities of traditionalist Catholics, and praised the monarchy. Lamennais was scornful of the whole effort. It was too moderate. It did not see the full implications of the revolution. It compromised its liberalism by its affection for the Bourbons. For Lamennais, the principles of liberal Catholicism admitted of no qualification. They involved total departure from recent Church policies, though Lamennais did claim sanctions in older Church traditions. It was Lamennais, not the *Correspondant* group, that won public attention. After 1830, in fact, the *Correspondant* had to suspend operations because of the support that the more radical Mennaisians had drawn away from them.

Lamennais brought both brilliance and rigidity to his liberal Catholicism. He gave it an unprecedented impulsion and attracted comment from all over Europe. The bishop of New York in 1829 appealed to him to send his liberal disciples to the United States. Lamennais' reputation drew Catholic attention; his intellectual power compelled liberal attention. Yet he created a system of liberal Catholicism that ultimately attracted few Catholics and few liberals. He would not compromise. He had discovered the true principles and would announce them, confident that they would ultimately prove victorious.

By the end of the Restoration Lamennais, firm in his hatred of the existing regime, felt that the monarchy was plunging deeper and deeper into despotism. The revolution that he had long considered inevitable now became eminently desirable. He saw that the future belonged to the democratic principles that were penetrating the minds of the masses; and he realized that these principles could bring great good. The old order was doomed; Lamennais' only wish was that which Christ had expressed to Judas: "*Quod facis, fac citius.* . . . "Whatever you do, do it quickly.'"[9]

Society had become, for Lamennais, a vast battlefield on which the forces of despotism and of anarchy contended. On one side were the Gallicans and monarchists, who wished to free the arbitrary will of the king from all restraints.* Against this, Lamennais urged liberalism. He wrote in 1829 that

liberalism, considered in its universal and permanent aspects, is nothing but the invincible desire for liberty inherent in Christian nations, which cannot endure an arbitrary or purely human government.[12]

But Lamennais still feared the idea of untrammeled individual sovereignty. The one hope for society was in the union of the principle of order with true liberty, that is, the establishment of liberty under Church guidance. Lamennais now saw the Church not only as guarantor of social stability, but also as the infallible depository of the divine laws of justice by which governments had to rule if they were to be legitimate. God wanted justice on earth as well as in heaven. The Church could bring justice by releasing the people from obedience to any sovereign who rejected God's tutelage. Hence the Church not only balanced liberty with order; it also ensured liberty.

To fulfill its modern role, the Church had to prepare itself among the people. It had to separate its fortunes from those of the doomed government, which was oppressing the Church anyway. The people, the real power in modern society, could be won back to religion only by persuasion, not by force. Instead of seeking political honors and power, the Church should work to win mankind in a free competition of ideas. To do so, Catholics should deal with modern minds. They should abandon their ignorance, their narrow scholasticism, and study the needs of contemporary society. The Church could attain its proper ascendance over modern

* See Appendix A, 11.

minds and become once more the center of all learning only
by utilizing modern discoveries in science, history, and other
fields. Most of all, the Church had to show the liberals that
Christianity was compatible with true liberalism. It had to
prove that it accepted and even encouraged the true principles of the revolution.

In less than a decade, Lamennais had moved from an
ultraconservative to a liberal position—and he was on the
verge of becoming radical. There were two points of conti-
nuity in his attitudes: he still believed that Catholicism was
socially necessary and that there was danger in the forces of
revolution. But before, he had seen the Church as a force to
expel the revolution from society; now he asked it to adopt
the main revolutionary principles and guide them to an
orderly and stable realization. He asserted vigorously that a
major effort at modernization was necessary if the Church
was to fulfill its mission.

Lamennais began to bend every effort to lead in the
modernization process. His writings, an important aspect of
this project, were intended to convert both Catholics and
liberals to his views. He published a major work on Church-
state relations in 1829. He wrote numerous pamphlets and
engaged in a bitter, published debate with the Archbishop
of Paris, Quélen, who had criticized Lamennais' presump-
tion "to erect his own opinions as dogmas" and "to shake
society itself by doctrines which sow defiance and hatred
between sovereigns and subjects."[11] This was a representative statement of the French hierarchy's view of Lamennais'
activities. Lamennais, knowing he was right, knowing it was
vital either to convert the hierarchy or to wean Catholics
away from it, wrote an exceptionally vigorous rebuttal. And
privately he noted, a short time later: "Our incorrigible
bishops are throwing themselves into battle, with their
ridiculous pronouncements in hand, and seem to have
pledged to bury the last remains of Christianity in France

under the trembling throne of the tyranny which is destroying them."[12] Defying ecclesiastical discipline in the overriding interests of saving religion, Lamennais clearly regarded himself as a final authority in the French Church.

In 1830 the Mennaisian movement founded a new journal, the *Revue Catholique*. The old *Mémorial* continued, but it needed a less philosophical supplement. The *Revue* demanded the full independence of the Church, especially in education. It urged social and political liberty, but in good order; and for this it sought a union of all good men on the basis of political principles fixed in divine law. Finally, and this was a new note, it stated that only Catholic principles of charity and equality before God could end the exploitation of the many by the few in the modern economic system. The *Revue*, a first step toward the provision of a regular outlet for Mennaisian political views, was evidence of Lamennais' new concern for consistent contact with political affairs and of the progress of the movement generally.

Lamennais was active outside of politics, for his program of religious rejuvenation was broad. His other principal aim was to modernize and revivify Catholic teaching and intellectual activities. Toward this end, beginning in 1827, he discreetly circulated appeals for young Catholics to come to Brittany for education under his direction. In 1828 a formal organization was established, the *Congrégation de Saint-Pierre*, which was meant to be a religious order adapted to modern times. It sought to preach loyalty to the Holy See, to defend the Church against the government, and to oppose the dangerous doctrines of individual reason by an extensive Catholic science founded on Mennaisian principles. Lamennais was the superior general of the order, but his brother, Jean, was largely responsible for its administration. The principal function of the order was education, both at La Chesnaie and at Malestroit, where a novitiate was established. Young men were trained to Catholicize their century by understanding it. They were encouraged to discuss contemporary politics, and learned at least three foreign languages. History, literature, mathematics, and the natural sciences were taught, in addition to theology and Mennaisian philosophy. With this education, given to as many novices as they could handle, Lamennais and his co-workers hoped to make a beginning in the reconquest of men's minds by Catholicism.

Through all his efforts, political and educational, Lamennais at the end of the Restoration was gathering a following about him. Some men, attracted by the reputation of the man they called master, drifted to him out of a desire to do something effective for Catholicism. Others were actively solicited, either by Lamennais or by one of his followers. The result was a rather extensive, though loosely organized, personnel for the Mennaisian movement. The talents assembled were considerable. Some of the disciples had organizing abilities, which Lamennais himself lacked. Gerbet was of course one of these, but there were others. The abbé Combalot, who joined the movement in 1827, was a great fundraiser; by 1828 he had raised 17,000 francs. In 1830 Charles de Coux volunteered his services to Lamennais for the defense of Church and society. A self-taught student of economics, he had worked out on his own the idea that only Catholicism could prevent the enslavement of modern industrial workers. Through contact with De Coux, Lamennais himself gradually became aware of industrial problems. The Mennaisian movement, now well beyond the sole influence of Lamennais, had attracted a large share of the most able young men in the French Church. Many were to assume leading positions in the Church in later decades. All now seemed inspired with a zeal to modernize religion either intellectually or politically or both. Inevitably there was diversity of opinion in this large group. Some, attracted by the Mennaisian philosophy, were royalist in politics; others, drawn to liberal Catholicism, had little contact with that philosophy. Although some of these differences were to be important later on, at this time the crucial point was that Lamennais, because he stood for a radical adaptation of the Church to modern times, served as a unifying force.

The enthusiasm of the disciples for Lamennais was intense. He compelled them by his reputation and by his personal kindness and consideration. Combalot wrote: "not all the prophets of the house of Israel have perished in the ruins of our temples. . . . The cause of God has found once more a defender worthy of it."[13] Another disciple hurried to Brittany, filled with "a perspective well beyond the hopes my imagination had conceived."[14] The ardor, even devotion, that Lamennais could inspire was a continuing feature of the movement developing around him.

Probably the most important addition to the Mennaisian movement was the adherence of Henri-Baptiste Lacordaire in 1830. Lacordaire proved to be one of the leading figures in liberal Catholicism; his attachment to Lamennais, though not so deep as that of some, is illustrative of the pull the Breton priest exercised. Lacordaire had been a liberal since his youth; he was not against the monarchy, but wanted a constitutional, parliamentary regime. At first he considered the Church an obstacle to liberty; gradually, however, he found in Catholicism certain immutable principles that were essential to limit the sovereignty of man. He became a priest in 1827. Lacordaire believed, then, that society needed both religion and liberty. However, he soon discovered that he was trying to unite two things that almost everyone else deemed irreconcilable, and he was suspected by his fellows because of his political views. He served as almoner, or chaplain, in a college, and through this association became convinced of the ineffectiveness of the Church's relations with the state. The only solution was separation of Church and state and a union of the cause of Catholicism and liberty.

Lacordaire, utterly discouraged by 1830 by his own position and that of the Church, intended to go to New York, where the Church was free. To do this, however, it was desirable to visit Lamennais first, since so many of the French priests in New York were disciples of the master. Gerbet and others had been trying for years to attract Lacordaire to their ranks, but Lacordaire had consistently rejected their overtures. He disagreed with Lamennais' philosophy and found his political views "exaggerated."[15] Now, reconsidering, Lacordaire saw that he and Lamennais were in basic agreement on the Church-state issue. He even came to accept Lamennais' philosophy, though without much enthusiasm. Lamennais, he wrote, was "after all . . . the only great man in the Church of France," and his school "the only Catholic school that is working today, and at things that show some progress every day."[16] Finally, Lacordaire visited Lamennais and accepted his tutelage; soon he was addressing the master as "my very good father"[17] and was busily seeking supporters for the Mennaisian contingent in the United States.

Lamennais exercised a compelling power over his disciples. Much of the strength of the Mennaisian movement lay in the deep attachment to the master; associates clung to Lamennais despite bitter criticism from other segments of the French Church, often despite substantial disagreement with Lamennais' political views. Lacordaire attributed a sort of magic to the impression Lamennais made on him; after he had broken with him, he professed not to understand how he could have joined him in the first place. Many disciples stressed the dictatorial character of the master; one noted that Lamennais granted great affection, but only on condition that the disciple yield his mind completely, to be filled with Mennaisian thought. Lamennais certainly did hate contradiction. But he did not force himself on his associates and he urged his disciples to develop their own particular talents to the fullest. He maintained intellectual ascendancy over those drawn to him, by the brilliance and vigor of his views. He also had a personal ascendancy, based on his sincere, somewhat paternal affection for his disciples; and he drew great strength from the devotion which they returned. Finally, as Lacordaire had noted, he served as a beacon for all who were dissatisfied with the official position of the Church. He was a great man; he was right about many of the evils of the day; and, whether right or not, he had vigorous notions about alternative policies. He seemed, in short, to see the modern world for what it really was.

The Mennaisian movement was loosely organized; it was united by common passions, not common institutions. Its members shared a deep intellectual and personal loyalty to Lamennais and a vital concern for the revival of Catholicism. A spirit and energy had been roused eager both to defend and to prod the Church in all its relations with modern society.

The Church was about to face a crisis. Its own position had been fading, and by now so was the position of the regime on which it depended. Yet there was little sign of any change in official policies, either within the French hierarchy or at Rome. There continued to be considerable complacency about the gains the Church had made. Yet there seemed to be no viable alternative to the existing policies. Without attachment to the government, the Church would be unprotected against the attacks of liberals and skeptics. If Catholic political and intellectual traditions could not be preserved, what was there to cling to in these uncertain times? It was recognized that there were novel forces beyond the Church's control. For most Catholic leaders this recognition was one more good reason to turn to the past. It was not clear that the traditions of a sympathetic monarchy were dead. With just a bit of wishful thinking, one could hope that the liberal forces could be defeated. There seemed to be no reason to experiment with novelty in an age in which most political and intellectual changes seemed directly hostile to religion.

But the French Church was split by 1830. The officials of the Church—the power of the Church—stood on the side of the established order. But they could not take the whole Church with them. Around Lamennais, an extraordinary movement had developed. Here was a simple priest who sought to lay down policy for the whole Church. His organizations had no authorization from the hierarchy. He even wrote directly against leading bishops. Inevitably he was regarded with suspicion by the prelates, even apart from his doctrines. But the man had power. It was not known how much numerical support he had in the Church, but he seemed to draw some of the most vigorous young minds. His writings continued to be purchased in substantial quantities. In Belgium a movement was growing that seemed to confirm many Mennaisian views. Finally, the position of the papacy on this new movement remained undefined. Leo XII died in 1829; neither of his successors was to have his sympathy for Lamennais. Leo, though intensely conservative, had esteemed Lamennais for his defense of the papacy and of religion. Stories circulated that he had a picture of Lamennais in his chambers and even that he had secretly made Lamennais a cardinal. There was good reason, of course, for Rome to give some support to Lamennais, if only as a check on the Gallicanism of the French hierarchy. As long as papal ambiguity continued with regard to the Mennaisian movement, Lamennais would not be operating without some possible support from above. For this reason as well as because of the strength of his personality, Lamennais was a force by 1830.

The bulk of that year constituted a period of watchful waiting for Lamennais. The policies of the French Church annoyed him increasingly. Reports of some Gallican statement or an anticlerical attack would throw him into a rage. The continuing criticisms of the Catholic and legitimist press bothered him. But for the most part he devoted himself to teaching and to the elaboration of a new general philosophy. His liberalism was growing stronger. Overjoyed at the union of Catholics and liberals in Belgium, he believed that the same movement would soon develop in France. "People tremble before liberalism; well, Catholicize it and Society will be reborn," he wrote.[18] But he realized that nothing could be done yet. Catholics would have to see their need for liberty; the pope must recognize his true duties. There was no point in saying more, for only new disasters, new persecutions, could teach Catholics their role in modern society. He was confident, though, that this time would come soon; a new era was dawning. In hopeful impatience he became prophetic; on the last day of June 1830 he wrote:

I am quite persuaded that nothing henceforward can turn aside the catastrophe which threatens us; and in truth I do not even know whether we should not desire it rather than fear it, for nothing tolerable can result from the present situation. There is today in all Europe one internal obstacle to life [the monarchy], and this obstacle will disappear only after a series of crises.[19]

CHAPTER IV

THE *"AVENIR"* MOVEMENT

The Revolution of 1830, bringing crisis and confusion to the whole Church, altered the relationship between the liberal Catholics and the French Church once more. Old Church policies could nowhere be continued unchanged. Yet interpretations of the new situation varied greatly. Some Catholics could not accept the new regime because of their affection for the departed Bourbon monarchy. Others, including the officials of the Church, reluctantly adhered to the Orelanist monarchy and sought to restore as much of their old relationship with the government as possible. The liberal Catholics, led by Lamennais, tried to use the revolution to force a radical alteration in the orientation of the Church. For Lamennais himself, the revolution was a sign that new forms of action were needed to further his cause.

The whole Church was affected by the revolution. Even the papacy was touched by revolts in the Papal States. The general reaction of the Church was to cling to past policies. But there was now a more organized and compact liberal Catholic movement than ever before, and it urged innovation. A clash seemed inevitable.

On July 27, 1830, the abbé Godefroy was giving a dinner for some notables of his parish, near Paris, when he heard bells sounding and saw young men carrying tricolor flags in the street. The good priest was old and his stomach was full; in the excitement, he became ill and died of congestion almost immediately.

The Revolution of 1830 was not fatal to the rest of the French clergy, but it came as a great shock. For the legitimists, the change in regime was itself profoundly disturbing. Several bishops doubted that they should give their oath of loyalty to the new regime, as was required of all state employees, including the churchmen. The hierarchy as a whole consulted the pope on this matter and received firm advice to take the oath. A few lower churchmen, including some professors of theology, did refuse their adherence and quit their jobs in preference. But the greater part of the clergy saw no profit in even tacit resistance to the state.

Naturally the sentiment for the legitimist regime was not gone. None of the bishops felt the affection for, or the emotional loyalty to, Louis-Philippe that they had maintained for the Bourbons. Several churchmen lent their churches to legitimist ceremonies; a legitimist mass in Paris in 1831 occasioned a major riot. And the active legitimists themselves, though laymen, were Catholics. All this created the impression that the Church was actively committed to the legitimist cause. The liberal press played up the idea of legitimist-Catholic association, to rouse anger against both its traditional enemies. During the first year after the revolution, then, it was not entirely clear whether the Church had abandoned active advocacy of legitimism. This was the source of much anger on the part of Lamennais and his colleagues.

In retrospect, however, it seems obvious that the Church still had no alternative to a policy of loyalty to the state. The government still granted funds to and made appointments in the Church. The pope still believed political ties were vital, a belief confirmed when he had to rely on Austrian support to suppress the revolution in the Papal States. The Church accepted the new regime in France, and prelates counseled loyalty and urged disinvolvement with politics. The intention was not only to avoid annoying the government but also to refrain from active commitment to it.

The position of the Church was complicated by both popular and official attacks. As Lamennais had predicted, the revolution was as much against the Church as against the Restoration government. During the revolutionary week in Paris, churches had to remain closed. For some time after, it was unsafe for a priest to appear in the streets in clerical garb. In Paris the revolution brought to the surface much of the hatred for the Church that had been developing over the years.

The revolution brought changes in government policies toward the Church. From the revised constitutional Charter was removed the reference to Catholicism as religion of state; it was termed instead the religion professed by the majority of Frenchmen. The Charter also promised laws granting liberty of association, of the press, and of instruction; the exact bearing of this on the Church was unknown, but there it was believed that a truly liberal regime would be installed, forcing further changes in the relationship of Church and state. On the practical level, the budget of the Church was scaled down drastically. The ministries of religion and education were given at first to anticlerical laymen rather than to members of the hierarchy. Initial appointments of new bishops naturally went to men loyal to the regime, and therefore often to men of dubious qualifications from the viewpoint of the Church. Anti-Catholic teachers had their jobs restored. The police investigated and closed down a number of religious houses, in various parts of France, because they had never been authorized by the government. Religious emblems and slogans were removed from courts of law. Louis-Philippe himself carefully avoided any official contact with religious ceremonies. Perhaps most important, the government tolerated popular manifestations against religion.

Many of the men running the government were anti-Catholic or indifferent to religion. A few Protestants were prominent in the new regime. Beyond this, the government recognized that a relatively harsh policy was necessary for political reasons in the early 1830's. Popular sentiment against the Church ran high. Leading newspapers exercised vigilance in their supervision of Church-state relations. When Louis-Philippe used the word "Providence" in speaking to the Chamber of Deputies, a moderate paper attached to the regime warned the public that the government was heading toward mysticism.

A revolutionary mood persisted in several cities for at least four years. Many elements of the lower class were surprised and angry that they had won so little by their revolutionary effort. Riots and strikes were frequent and bitter. Since the government needed all the support it could get, obviously there was no point in making matters worse by undue friendliness to the Church; this would create further popular outrage. The fact that the Church had been so manifestly attached to the Restoration made it an uncertain political quantity. The state did not seek war with the Church; it did not desire really fundamental change in its relations with Catholicism. But the government sought to divert the revolutionary excitement toward the Church. Attacks on the Church were far better than attacks on the regime.

Liberal Catholics thought that the new conditions demanded separation of Church and state. At first they looked to the government as essentially liberal; they had long believed that liberalism meant Church-state separation. As actual government hostility became more pronounced, this seemed one more vital reason for separation. Yet the Church hierarchy could not agree. For all the grievances that the prelates had against the government, for all the bitterness of their relations with state officials, there still seemed to be no adequate reason for an open break. A break would only increase official persecution of the Church, and the Church would be without funds and support to meet the attack. The hierarchy was convinced that the old policy of reliance on the state need not be altered. The Church could win more gains by pressing the government from within than by open feuding. The French Church had already suppressed its active legitimism in the interests of self-protection. Now it accepted the hardships the new regime imposed.

The liberal Catholics could not understand this position. Yet the whole weight of Church tradition in France lay behind it. And in many respects the position was later justified by the further evolution of the regime. After the first, confused period, the July Monarchy, becoming more friendly to the Church, increased the state religious budget and reduced the harassments of Church activities. The Restoration relationship of Church and state was never re-established, but a working agreement did develop, although well after the period under discussion.

For both Church leaders and the liberal Catholics, the postrevolutionary period was complicated by the continuing popular attacks on the Church. Because of the new press freedom, a variety of anti-Catholic publications were published. Plays and books ridiculed the Church. Pamphlets appeared with such enticing titles as "The Woman's nightshirt and gallant correspondence found in the oratory of the archbishopric of Paris."[1] Liberal newspapers seized on every opportunity to attack the Church. The public mood seemed decidedly hostile. Riots occurred. In early 1831 the palace of the archbishop of Paris was burned to the ground, and the old royal Church, Saint-Germain-l'Auxerrois, was sacked. Public crosses were overturned or destroyed in several parts of France. Churches were pillaged in Lyons, Lille, Nîmes, Angoulême, and elsewhere.

Judgments of churchmen on this situation differed. For the prelates, popular hostility was one more reason to maintain tested policies and rely on the state. There was little to do but to wait until the movement subsided. For the liberals, the riots were a clear sign of the tragic gulf between Church and society. They underscored the need for a reorientation of the Church away from conservative politics and toward fruitful contact with the people of France.

All major segments of the Church recognized the revolution and some of its implications, for the changes in government policy and the altered popular mood were undeniable. Yet opinions on the proper policies in this situation varied sharply. Disagreement quickly led to a sort of civil war within the French Church. The revolution sharpened positions on both sides, creating a mood of tension and uncertainty that complicated intelligent debates. The very weakness of the Church made internal dispute seem almost treasonous. The question was which side was betraying the true interests of Catholicism.

The revolution came as no surprise to Lamennais.* He was in Brittany at the time and so missed the excitement of direct contact with the revolutionary fervor, but he was immediately enthusiastic. At last his prophecies had been fulfilled; the revolution was a justifiable reaction against an arbitrary government and the inauguration of a new era of liberty, both for the Church and for the whole society. Lamennais sensed a great opportunity here to purify Church politics and to bring about the union of Catholicism and liberty on which both depended.

Lamennais also saw dangers in the new situation. There was the threat of renewed attack on the Church; there was constant danger of anarchy or tyranny resulting from revolutionary chaos; and there was the possibility that the revolu-

* See Appendix A, 12–13.

tion itself had not gone far enough, that its logical conclusion had not been attained. All three of these problems preoccupied Lamennais from the first. Together, they guided his activities for the next year.

The sense that the revolution was incomplete was to set Lamennais apart from all but a handful of political extremists. This was not clear until later, for Lamennais did not yet express his views publicly and his views were more fully developed by later events. However, from the first there was a fear that the era of ferment was not over, that a truly revolutionary society, a society really constructed in the principles of the revolution and a society that was therefore stable, had yet to be achieved. Particularly, Lamennais was disturbed that a new monarchy was installed by the leaders of the July rising. His sense of the logic of the revolution—a sense that was so often prophetic—told him that monarchy and modern society were incompatible. He wrote in August:

You are completely right, my dear friend; sooner or later we must end up with the Republic; I mean the Republic de jure, for we already have one in fact. And as for a long time perhaps no other government will be possible in France, I would prefer, for the tranquillity of the immediate future, greater harmony in the institutions that are being established; for anything opposed to the republican spirit can neither endure nor be changed without new shocks which might be extremely dangerous.[2]

Within a few months Lamennais was to become a republican by conviction. At present he was a republican, as before he had been a liberal, from a sense of inevitability. The belief in the necessity for a radically new society was already present.

The more pressing problems, however, concerned the relations between Catholics and liberals. Lamennais saw that some of the revolutionary factions might try to destroy the Church. Catholics had to unite in self-defense, but through the full acceptance of liberty. Through liberty they could save the Church and accommodate it to the modern world. And in so doing, they would provide the foundation for a new social order. For the broader danger, the danger in any revolutionary situation, was social chaos; and liberalism by itself, as Lamennais had always believed, lacked a principle of order. Only Catholicism could provide this. It was vitally necessary to unite Catholics and true liberals in the joint defense of liberty and order. To bring about this essential union, to eliminate prejudices on both sides, Lamennais felt that he had "an imperious duty" to enter the world of politics.[3] He was optimistic about his chances:

By far the most numerous party [is composed] of those men who are disposed to unite for the maintenance of order, on a wide basis of liberty. What they lack is something to draw them together, an organization which they have not yet been able to create, and which is held back by the remnants of old prejudices and suspicions; it is to this party that all the clergy, with the exception of some incorrigible Gallicans, will soon belong.[4]

At first Lamennais had to content himself with expressing his views through the two Mennaisian periodicals. But neither appeared frequently enough to serve as an active political organ. Soon after the revolution, however, Gerbet was invited to cooperate with a new daily paper designed to defend the rights guaranteed to the Church by the Charter. Gerbet immediately informed Lamennais of the plan "to establish a paper which would defend both religion and liberty."[5] Lamennais was enthusiastic and the newspaper was organized in September. Other Mennaisians were called to the effort, and the two other periodicals were discontinued in favor of concentration on this new project. The first issue appeared only on October 16. The paper was called the *Avenir*—the Future—and its motto was "God and Liberty."

Lamennais, excited about the paper, helped push it into publication before an adequate staff or financial base had been established. He came to Paris from Brittany in mid-September, eager to get into action at last. He even transferred the *Congrégation de Saint-Pierre* to a school near Paris, where he himself took up residence at the invitation of one of its directors. Lamennais was fully committed to this new project, and in turn his prestige gave the newspaper an immediate impact and importance. Both at the time and later, it proved easy to identify the paper with his name alone and to praise or damn it accordingly.

Lamennais' relationship to the paper was, however, complex. Never good at administrative work, he was by no means solely responsible for managing the *Avenir*. Even the bulk of the writing was done by others. Throughout most of the *Avenir*'s existence, Lamennais did not live in Paris; and his health was bad. He was working on a vast new general philosophy and lectured on this frequently, so he had little time for the writing of newspaper articles. Further, despite his great interest in journalism, he lacked the temperament for commenting on daily events or dealing with minor editorial quarrels. He wrote when he was moved to great anger or, most commonly, under the impulse of some new idea. His more important articles appeared in clusters, as he sought to develop a novel theory. He could not carry the newspaper alone. And precisely because he was spurred by a general philosophy, his approach differed from that of his collaborators.

The interests of the other editors of the *Avenir* varied widely. De Coux wrote a number of articles, primarily on economic issues. Gerbet did some writing until his own health failed in 1831. Lacordaire changed his mind about going to America and, on Gerbet's invitation, joined the editorial board instead. He did not need to go abroad to realize his ideas on the Church and society. A major contributor of the daily material for the *Avenir*, he sought out facts, discussed daily events, and engaged in lively polemics with other papers. His particular interest was always in Church-state relations. Unlike Lamennais, he did not speculate about the proper structure of society as a whole. But he was sincerely interested in attracting liberals to Catholicism and freeing the Church from state interference; on this basis, at least, he could devote himself to one aspect of what Lamennais himself sought.

Many other contributors were attracted to the paper. Several Belgians wrote occasional articles. The Baron d'Eckstein wrote on political affairs, though he ultimately found the paper too radical. Of the later additions to the staff of the *Avenir*, by far the most important was Count Charles de Montalembert.

Montalembert was twenty years old in 1830. He had long maintained an interest both in Catholicism and in liberty. He once signed a pact in blood pledging himself to God and liberty. As this act might imply, Montalembert was capable of more enthusiasm than precision in his political thought. He could be swept away into radical statements, and the excitement of the *Avenir* stirred him to extremes many times. He early developed an almost filial affection for Lamennais that clouded his political judgment. Despite all this, however, Montalembert was the most conservative of the *Avenir*'s leading editors. He praised liberty, but abhorred some of the consequences of liberalism. He was opposed to all egalitarian tendencies and believed that monarchy and especially the aristocracy were vital, civilizing forces. Unlike Lamennais, then, he did not look forward to further revolutions in society. Unlike Lacordaire, he did not confine himself to Church-state issues. However, he used the same terms as both these men, though the word "liberty" did not necessarily mean the same thing to him.

Despite differences of view, Montalembert regarded the *Avenir* as the only real hope for the Church and for liberty in France. He had been very disturbed by the July revolution. Although he welcomed it as a just defense against despotism, he was soon revolted by the excesses of the revolutionaries. He felt real sympathy for the fallen Bourbon house and feared that the revolution would destroy the social hierarchy of which he was a part. When he read the first issues of the *Avenir,* however, he felt that he had found the answer to his dilemma. Here was the alliance of which he had dreamed. Here was a chance to defend liberty as he understood it. In early November Montalembert went to see Lamennais, and was entranced by his views on the need to free the Church from the state. But, frightened by Lamennais' republicanism, which he could not share, Montalembert decided at first to contribute only occasional articles. Soon he was drawn into regular service, not because of a change of views but because he yearned for excitement and combat. And, like so many of his contemporaries, he believed that only Lamennais could "do something valuable for Catholicism, and that without him everything would be pale and impotent."[6]

Conceived in haste, inadequately financed, the *Avenir* was, then, launched haphazardly. Its editors were young and inexperienced. Its presumed leader was seldom present. The staff evinced real divergence of interest. The whole effort was to fail within thirteen months; yet the *Avenir* movement was important. For all its incoherence, it presented some of the basic doctrines of liberal Catholicism for the first time. It revolutionized Catholic journalism by showing the utility of the daily press. It forced liberals to define their position on the Church by using their own terms. Most important, the *Avenir* forced the Church to define its attitude toward liberty. The founding of the paper began three years of intense debate within the Church. None of the editors emerged unchanged from their experience, and several were to go on to important work later. Liberal Catholicism itself was altered. Its assumptions were more clearly stated, yet the limits of its activity were made more rigid. The Church, too, was changed, and was set upon a path of explicit conservatism that continued for half a century. Lamennais, the leader of the whole movement, was finally forced to choose between the Church and society.

It is vital to note that Lamennais did not direct the *Avenir* in any simple way, that there were differences, though largely unrecognized, between his views and those of his collaborators. It is vital to note that Lamennais himself regarded the *Avenir* as only one weapon in his campaign for social and religious reform. He continued to believe in the importance of a complete philosophical alternative to the doctrines of individual reason and spent much time developing and teaching his system. Still, Lamennais did provide the basic orientation for the *Avenir*. He was dutifully consulted on all major issues. Whatever he wrote was given great prominence; and his articles treated the most sweeping subjects, thus setting a tone for the more specific commentary of the daily paper. The major editors felt that they were working under Lamennais' direction and if they did not share all his interests, they were too busy at the time to notice potential discrepancies. Most important, Lamennais felt fully responsible for the project. He participated directly in the major successes and failures of the movement, and his own views were altered as a result. His passionate devotion to the cause of the *Avenir* led him to basic changes in his own life and philosophy.

Lamennais' social theories changed greatly through his association with the *Avenir;* he became progressively more radical. He now had to think more specifically about politics; he tended to carry through earlier lines of thought to their logical conclusion. Much that had been suggested before in private correspondence was now spelled out in public, and with the logical passion, the concern for systematic truth, which Lamennais always applied to his published writings. Furthermore, the attacks on the *Avenir* impelled Lamennais to rethink his views on the French Church and, ultimately, on the papacy; criticism was always likely to spur his mind. Simply being near Paris, near the center of such feverish political activity, obviously affected him. The aftermath of the revolution of 1830, in France and elsewhere, contributed to his excitement about the prospects of social change. All of Europe seemed on the verge of revolutionary transformation. Lamennais could see the shape of the new society more clearly now, and he grew less patient with anything standing in the way of progress. Lamennais did not coolly direct the *Avenir* movement along pre-established lines. He developed yet another stage, the final stage really, in his political thought, and the *Avenir* was the vehicle and expression of this change.

Lamennais' central concern in the early months of the *Avenir*'s existence was the need to defend order through a union of Catholics and liberals. This was a massive project in itself. It involved defense of the Church by new means, by the active use of legal liberties. It involved working with non-Catholics and converting them, not to Catholicism, but to a common purpose in the protection of liberty and order. This would set the basis for a new, stable society, but this new society was not spelled out. Lamennais was really preoccupied with the need to avoid both the anarchy and the tyranny of the earlier revolution, and he was not sure that even this was possible: "The only means of stopping anarchy, if we can, or at least of reducing it, is to organize an active resistance by uniting, by organizing all those who fear it."[7] But in 1831, Lamennais began talking of the necessity of further revolutions and of the possibility of a new and more perfect level of human society. His later views tended to drift away from the more prosaic and Church-centered interests of his colleagues on the *Avenir*. Ultimately, these new views were to drive Lamennais from the Church. To Lamennais, however, they represented the true meaning of liberal Catholicism. And he continued to represent liberal Catholicism in France. His new radicalism was intensely personal, but it colored the fate of the whole liberal Catholic movement.

The decisive changes in Lamennais' views were completed during the spring of 1831. He wrote his brother Jean on June 26: "I have finished four long articles which will soon appear ... in the *Avenir*. They are important in showing the development of my doctrine, because of the new ideas in them, ideas which alter the appearance of several questions."[8] It is essential to divide the presentation of the doctrines of the *Avenir* into two sections. The first contains the central doctrines of the newspaper, those shared by all the editors. These were the doctrines to which Lamennais devoted himself in the first months of the movement. These were the doctrines that dominated most of the editorials and activities of the movement. Lamennais drew only a few colleagues, and only partially, into his later, more radical ideas. These were the ideas of a prophet: they painted a society based on democracy and the quest for economic justice. They were the ideas of a dreamer: they portrayed Catholicism leading the movement for political and economic reform. They represented at once the completion of Lamennais' social philosophy and the separation between Lamennais and the mainstream of nineteenth-century liberal Catholicism.

The basis of all the ideas of the *Avenir* was the deep sense of social change* that had long dominated Lamennais. An invincible force in society impelled change and progress. Whether men wished to or not, they had to yield to this force, which was divine: God was working in the world and acted through terrestrial events. This was the source of the "precipitous movement" that was sweeping over the world.[9] This was the source of the irresistibility of change.

The past was dying, a new kind of society being born. The

---

* See Appendix B, 2.

Bourbons had failed because they had not done what the times required; hence the need for a revolution, to clear the way for the social plans of God. The revolution would continue until men learned to build not in the image of the past but in the spirit of the future, not according to dreams but according to the realities of change. The Revolution of 1830 was one important step toward the future; therefore, and this had to be stressed for French Catholics, it was here to stay. The results of the revolution would, moreover, be ultimately beneficial. The revised Charter, particularly, was a true expression of the needs of the times. If properly used, if accepted and utilized by Catholics, it could be the basis for social peace: "The Charter . . . is the goal of all our desires, the object of all our hopes. It is our second religion."[10]

The most pressing problem of the new social order was the establishment of the proper relationship between Church and state. All the editors agreed with Lamennais that the close link between Church and state during the Restoration had nearly destroyed the Church. The government had limited the divinely appointed activities of the Church, and the alliance had aroused popular hatred for the Church: "finding servitude near the altar, men became afraid of God.[11] The Revolution of 1830 both promised and required a welcome change. Catholicism was no longer the official religion; Lamennais felt that this could only mean that the Church was legally freed from state control. And this was not only a fact but a necessity. Catholics had to learn to use liberty to protect themselves against a potentially hostile regime. They had to learn to defend liberty as a precondition for obtaining popular favor, for Lamennais had long been convinced that the people would reject any institution that opposed liberty. And they had to embrace liberty in order to defend society itself; this would be the basis of that essential union of liberals and Catholics to preserve both liberty and order.

Lamennais and his colleagues therefore sought full separation of Church and state. This would, of course, help protect the Church against the hostility of the July revolutionaries, for, quite obviously, state interference was now likely to be directly harmful to the Church. But it was not only defense of Catholicism against a hostile government that the editors intended. The point was that any government, even one favorable to Catholicism, could aid religion only by adopting a policy of strict noninterference. France was a nation of divided beliefs. Any special favors to Catholicism would be despotic and would therefore do more harm than good; for the spirit of the age, this divine force for change, was against tyranny, and constraint could do nothing to advance the truth. Men had to be free to resolve religious problems, for they were accountable to God alone. Clearly the desire for separation of Church and state was not merely a tactical device to be used during a period of government hostility; it reflected a real belief in spiritual freedom.

This was a radical doctrine for the Church, and the editors knew it. There was no major religion on the continent that did not receive state support, no major state without an official or semi-official church. But in a revolutionary age neither tradition nor present practice had any essential relevance. Lamennais could not understand how any Catholic could deny the need for separation, given the recent experiences of the Church in France:

Imagine the future consequences of a situation which has already produced such damaging results. Religion administered like tariffs and taxes, the priesthood degraded, discipline ruined, teaching oppressed, the Church, in a word, deprived of its necessary independence, communicating with its leader with ever-increasing difficulty, and daily submitted more harshly to the whims of the temporal power, shaped by it to all its purposes, receiving everything from it, its pastors, its laws, even its doctrines: what is this, if not death?[12]

Against this prospect, Lamennais asserted the ultimate power of Catholic truth, once it was freed from the tutelage of the state. Religious liberty did not mean abandoning the effort to convert all men to Catholicism; rather, it was a precondition for conversion. No error could prevail over Catholicism in a free contest. If the Church gave up its political preoccupations, it could devote itself to the struggle. Essentially irrelevant political disputes would cease to be barriers to Catholic belief. As Lacordaire wrote:

Let this spiritual war be continued and ended by purely spiritual weapons. Truth is all-powerful. . . . We believe firmly that the development of modern intelligence will one day lead not only France but all of Europe to Catholic unity which, later and by a successive progress, attracting to it the rest of the human race, will constitute humanity by one and the same faith in one and the same spiritual society.[13]

Separation of Church and state undeniably meant the sacrifice of privileges. Without this, the state could claim the right to intervene in Church affairs. Priests should receive no special legal treatment; civil guarantees of clerical celibacy would have to be abandoned. Most important, the church must renounce state payments. The Church admittedly had a right to them, since they were compensation for confiscated lands. But what good was this abstract right when it served as a pretext for constant state interference? Far better to be poor, like the apostles, than to be oppressed. And the charity of the Catholic faithful would sustain the Church, as it did in Ireland and the United States. "We demand neither privileges nor favors, we want liberty,"[14] wrote one of the editors.

Lamennais and his colleagues did not hesitate to specify what liberty they wanted. They urged, for example, freedom from concordats of any kind. There was no need to spell out Church-state relations, and in practice the concordats were unfavorable to the Church. Of course, since the concordats were made with papal agreement, and since the editors professed unlimited submission to the pope, the criticism of the concordats was circumspect. But the principle remained clear: a concordat, implying some association between Church and state, was contrary to the Charter and therefore wrong. The editors blasted the idea of government appointment of bishops, as authorized by the Concordat of 1801. Separation of Church and state was essential in this area, all the more since many poor appointments were made in 1830 and 1831. If carried too far, the government could enslave the Church by appointing bishops favorable to the government. The final result would be a national church, obeying the state instead of the pope. Lamennais was particularly violent on this point, because it was central to religious freedom. In an article for which the government prosecuted him, he told Catholics:

The election of your chief pastors is in the hands of men who are only too justly suspect of planning the ruin of your faith. . . . The only remedy is the entire and absolute separation of church and state, [for] the intervention of the government in religious matters is altogether absurd and illegal.[15]

The Charter had proclaimed the freedom of education, and the *Avenir* demanded freedom of education as well as freedom of religion. Both involved the mind and spirit of man; governments should have no power over these. Education had an additional claim to liberty by virtue of a father's inalienable right to provide for his children as he saw fit. The *Avenir* constantly attacked the University monopoly, calling it unjust and, according to the Charter, illegal. It imposed state opinions on all students. And it was impious, for it condemned Catholic families either to leave their sons in ignorance or to send them to certain corruption. A state system obviously was legitimate. But it should exist in freedom, without monopoly; other systems should have equal rights beside it. If all beliefs could compete freely in teaching, truth would prevail.

The *Avenir* vigorously supported freedom of the press, another God-given outlet for communication. It could propagate the truth; it could serve as another field for the free combat of truth and error. So all censorship was opposed, then, even if it might act in the name of Catholicism. The *Avenir* defended both royalist and republican papers against government persecution, for the government, composed of fallible men, could not serve as the judge of truth and falsehood.

This attitude toward freedom was the essence of liberal Catholicism. Freedom for the Church was seen as a necessity for true religion and also as part of a general system of liberty. Merely defining the program, however, was not enough; means had to be found to achieve it.

The *Avenir* sincerely hoped for an alliance with French liberals; Lamennais particularly urged this as a political weapon. There was much talk of "new" liberals who sought equal liberty for all. A union with these men, even if they were Protestants or atheists, could bring into being the freedom that both groups desired. Such a union would benefit society as a whole. In a revolutionary era Catholics and liberals could join in a defense of order and property and of the solid gains of the Revolution of 1830. They could combat the forces of anarchy; they could keep the government on the right path. Going beyond these goals, the *Avenir* held that Catholicism was necessary for true liberty. Lamennais had long pointed out that non-Catholic freedom was simply the right of each man to do as he pleased. This view made man the judge of justice and injustice, and whoever could impose his personal ideas of justice on others would rule. Non-Catholic liberty would lead to a brutish society. True liberty was the right to do what was just, and only God could grant this.

To be free, man had to perceive justice; and since the Church was the interpreter of the divine law of justice, the Church was essential to liberty. Only when liberals realized this would they be able to build a durable society.

The idea of union with good liberals, then, had many facets. There were broad hopes for society and for liberty itself. There was also a firm realization that liberal support would be invaluable for the Church, as a defense against the attacks of the "older" liberals, whom the *Avenir* constantly assailed. The alliance with liberals was seen primarily as a necessity for the general reunion of Church and people. Lamennais firmly believed that the people had been driven from the Church because of its political conservatism. Yet the strength and salvation of Church and society clearly rested with the people. It was vital for the Church to draw the masses to it by divesting itself of political power and undue wealth. The priest should unite with the people, sharing their desires and needs. And, since humanity was progressing, the Church had to advance with it. It was senseless to perpetuate the gulf between the two forces.

Part of the *Avenir*'s liberal Catholicism was this appeal to true liberals. However, the editors sought their principal support from the body of French Catholics. Liberals made uncertain allies, because of the tradition of hostility to the Church. The *Avenir* looked to the defense of the Church above all, a cause that would interest few liberals. And even to win the liberals, attention had to be given to the policies of the Church. Catholics had to be convinced of the need for liberty before liberals could be expected to drop their old suspicions. For various reasons, then, the editors addressed themselves particularly to their co-religionists. Even Lamennais, whose interest in wooing the liberals was great, devoted most of his attention to winning Catholics from political attitudes he regarded as archaic.

As a first step, the *Avenir* told Catholics that the old attachment to legitimism was futile and harmful. A restoration of the Bourbons was impossible; Catholics should ally themselves with a political movement only in the interests of their religion, not because of devotion to a particular dynasty. The *Avenir* became steadily more vehement in its comments on the legitimists. At first it was conciliatory, claiming to understand the sympathies for the past. But as royalists stubbornly refused to abandon their views and still tried to involve Catholicism in their efforts, the tone changed. Bitterness reached a peak in February 1831, when a legitimist ceremony occasioned the sacking of the church of Saint-Germain. Lamennais, Gerbet, and Lacordaire united in stinging condemnations of the royalists for associating religion with a detested politics. Lamennais was particularly angry: "Break forever with men whose incorrigible blindness impedes this holy religion, who sacrifice their God to their king."[16] Other editors, notably Montalembert, tried to soften the effects of this blast. But the *Avenir*'s stand was clear: royalism must be abandoned in the interests of religion.

Beyond this, Catholics had to be trained in the use of liberty. They would have to learn to demand their rights under the Charter, rather than yield to persecution or demand government help. The *Avenir* not only explained what liberty was but also campaigned for its application. Here was the true political interest of the Church, for it would benefit the Church directly.

The *Avenir* constantly pointed out abuses of religious liberty by the government. They denounced government prohibitions of religious ceremonies; as long as these did not disturb public order, there was no reason to prevent them. They blasted the state for failing to provide police protection for Church buildings and crosses; protection of property was a matter of common right. It became increasingly clear that the government would not voluntarily grant true religious freedom. Catholics would have to obtain this by their own efforts.

The editors gently urged the pope to resist government interference and lead in the liberation of the Church. They told the episcopate to demand its rights and particularly to resist government appointment of bishops. But their chief hopes rested with the Catholic masses. Lamennais had long felt that the future of religion lay with the people, that the episcopacy had to be partially by-passed; now he sought to apply this view. Again and again he and his colleagues urged the Catholic faithful to awake, unite, and utilize the legal means provided by the Charter to defend their rights. Catholics should stop being passive cowards. If the 25 million Catholics of France unanimously demanded their rights, who would dare refuse them?

The ultimate hope was a real Catholic party: "Let no one be astonished at this word 'party'; the Catholics form the majority of the nation. . . ."[17] The *Avenir* urged Catholic voters to act according to their religious interest. They should demand pledges from all candidates to work for religious liberty and vote for the candidate who gave the firmest pledge. This would develop a wedge of votes that all parties would have to heed. This act should be a major aspect of the Catholics' defense of their own rights.

The final feature of the *Avenir's* liberal Catholicism, then, was a desire to change Catholic politics. The sterile attachment to irrelevant political causes must be dropped. The editors proposed a flexible stance, based on a firm desire for Catholic interests and, therefore, for liberty. Alliance with liberals in a common cause should be part of Catholic politics. In fact, Catholics were urged to become the principal defenders of liberty.

The editors of the *Avenir* were not content to enunciate their doctrines; they intended to apply them. They planned to lead in the campaign for freedom. As Lacordaire said, "Liberty is not given, it is taken."[18] And all the necessary legal means were available. The government might protest, but against the government Catholics could appeal both to the Charter and to the spirit of the times.

Lacordaire and Montalembert, who had the youth and enthusiasm for the effort, led a program of action that formed an important part of the *Avenir* movement. Lamennais approved of the program and was drawn in as leader of the whole project. The vigor of the project roused Lamennais, late in 1831, to formulate a new and broader plan of action to save society.

Understanding that publicity was a powerful weapon, the *Avenir* opened its columns to Catholic complaints against any government misconduct toward the Church. Letters poured in from priests and faithful all over France, listing grievances against the government. A letter from Nancy denounced army occupation of a seminary and a bishop's palace. The letter expressed the sentiment of many of the correspondents of the *Avenir:* "It is in you that true Catholics today put all their hopes when they are the victims of vile persecution."[19]

The *Avenir* sought to raise money for many religious causes. These campaigns aided the Church financially and also gave Catholics a sense of their united power. In 1831 almost 80,000 francs were raised to assist Irish Catholics in a famine year. French Catholics formed local committees, particularly in areas where the *Avenir* had been active in resisting government abuses. Even some legitimists gave assistance. Following this significant success, the editors opened several other subscriptions. In August 1831 they appealed for funds to rebuild the archbishopric of Paris. They collected more than a thousand francs in a week, but the archbishop asked that the effort be stopped; he preferred to negotiate with the government. Despite this setback, the idea of the voluntary-funds campaign had proved valuable.

Early in the project, the editors had realized that their activities would be more extensive and more effective if they had support from some sort of organization. They felt keenly the powerlessness of the individual against the modern state; oppression could be prevented only by the association of the oppressed. As early as October 1830, Lamennais had proposed a vast society of mutual assistance, open to all men of good will, without regard to political or religious opinions. The association would defend the rights of all; and it would be locally based, so the government could not easily attack it. This was too broad an idea, too remote from the Church, even to appeal to most of the other editors. But Lamennais did consider the possibility of a Catholic group for defense of the Church above all. By December many Catholics were urging such an organization, and several local groups had been formed to act on the *Avenir*'s principles. And in December Lamennais and Lacordaire were brought to trial, the implications of which determined the need for an association at last.

On November 26 and 27, 1830, the government seized issues of the *Avenir*. The first contained an article by Lacordaire blasting some recent episcopal nominations; the second featured the article by Lamennais denouncing government abuses of the Church. The government charged both men with exciting hatred and scorn of the government. The editors welcomed the trial as an opportunity to publicize their beliefs and they urged Catholics to report any new abuses so that these could be cited. They appealed for small contributions to defray costs and enlist active Catholic support. As a result, 18,726 people subscribed a total of 14,768 francs. Finally, Lamennais hired a liberal, Protestant lawyer for his defense, an active illustration of the sort of alliance of God and liberty that he intended.

The trial was a dramatic event. Lacordaire, who was a trained lawyer, spoke in his own behalf. Lamennais sat with his head bowed, pale, looking old and wrinkled; he spoke softly and briefly—only his flashing eyes showed the spark in the man. The government prosecutor treated both of the accused as simple agitators, fomentors of riots. Lamennais' lawyer, in contrast—and somewhat unfortunately as it turned out—portrayed Lamennais as the regenerator of Catholicism in modern times. Most important, the two editors were acquitted. Lamennais saw the whole episode as abundant vindication of his whole approach. His hatred of the July Monarchy was heightened, but his enthusiasm for relying on a combination of popular support and legal resistance was greatly heightened. In fact, in his excitement, he exaggerated the importance of the trial. But he and his colleagues were undeniably encouraged to press on in their dual effort to protect the Church against a hostile government and to arouse Catholic support for liberty.

The support the editors had received in the trial, combined with increasing realization that the government did not intend to relax its control over the Church, motivated the founding of the General Agency for the Defense of Religious Liberty. The Agency vowed to protect the clergy against abuse by bringing any and all cases to trial. It promised to support any school against all acts contrary to the liberty of teaching. And it pledged itself to defend the right of all Frenchmen to unite for any religious, charitable, or civilizing purpose. All these activities give evidence of Lamennais' influence. In practice, the Agency concentrated on Catholic problems; and it was able to obtain support from many who did not share the *Avenir's* political views. Even so, the Agency embodied several new principles. It was directed primarily against the government, seeking to use courts of law as the primary weapon; older Catholic groups had united against unofficial attacks by revolutionaries. It relied on laymen as much as on members of the clergy. Finally, the Agency tried to foster local groups all over France. The Agency was intended to express the new mood of Catholicism and to encourage Catholics to even greater activity.

The Agency conducted a number of cases in defense of the Church. Late in 1831 it defended a Trappist house in Brittany against expropriation by the government. It ultimately won the case, though the further demand that the prime minister be brought to trial as author of the crime against religious freedom was, of course, denied. At Aix a local military commander ordered a congregation of Capuchins not to appear publicly in religious garb. The Agency hastened to offer legal aid, though the Capuchins later decided they did not want trouble. In the spring of 1831 the government appointed the abbé Guillon Bishop of Beauvais. Guillon did not have an unblemished record as an ecclesiastic, and the *Avenir* was incensed. The Agency helped organize a petition by clergy in the diocese against the bishop. One hundred and twenty priests signed. Guillon resigned in September. Later he solaced himself by writing a three-volume denunciation of Lamennais. In these and in other cases, the Agency sought direct action against government interference in religious affairs.

One of the prime concerns of the Agency was education. The organization assisted in four cases in which the government prosecuted schools conducted without University authorization. A number of petitions against the state's monopoly of education were drafted. Several hundred based on the Agency model were sent to the Chamber of Deputies early in 1831, bearing a total of 16,617 signatures. The government ignored the petitions. Though the Agency was justly proud of having roused so many Catholics to action, it was clear that something else had to be done. In April the government ordered the priests of Marseilles to stop giving free

Latin lessons to their choirboys without University permission. This was the last straw. The Agency decided to set up its own school without authorization. If the school remained unmolested, the principles of freedom of education would be established. If the government did intervene, then the matter could be taken to court and argued on the basis of the Charter's grant of liberty of instruction.

The school opened on May 7 and the government closed it the next day. The resulting trial, involving Lacordaire and Montalembert, received great publicity. The whole Agency legal staff worked on it. The accused had ample opportunity to denounce the monopoly. They lost the case, but they had advanced their cause. By November 1831 Catholics in six cities planned to establish unauthorized schools under the general direction of the Agency.

The Agency lasted effectively for less than a year. It won few of its cases against the government; it caused no decisive changes in the position of the Church. Yet it had accomplished a great deal. Operating with a small staff and limited funds, in direct opposition to the government, it had challenged a variety of state abuses. Even when it could not win a legal case, the Agency's publicity had often forced the government to back down. Most important, the Agency had roused many Catholics in many areas to the active defense of the Church. Leaders of local affiliates, men who started free schools, even people who signed a petition or contributed to a charity appeal—all were working for the Church in new ways. Together they managed to give the Church of France a degree of independent activity unprecedented in previous decades.

Lamennais supported both the doctrines and the activities of liberal Catholicism. He wanted to free the Church from state control and to rouse Catholics in defense of their rights. If he wrote only occasionally, if he did not participate in the daily administration of the Agency, he helped determine basic lines of action and sponsored the major efforts. Nevertheless, his thinking went beyond that of the other editors of the *Avenir*. He was developing a plan for a total new society.* Liberal Catholicism was a key to this society, but it was not the only one.

The difference in orientation showed even in the view of Catholic association. Lamennais initially had suggested a broad organization, including non-Catholics and directed toward general liberal politics. He recognized that this was impractical, and actively planned and supported the more limited Agency that was created. However, in November 1831, when the *Avenir* suspended operations, he returned to his earlier idea. He now proposed an international union of liberals and Catholics. Catholics would lead in the effort, since they alone could establish true liberty. But all men who loved liberty could unite with them to create a new Europe. The union was to be founded on three basic principles. The spiritual part of society would be completely separate from the temporal; so there would be liberty of religion, of education, of the press. In the material sphere, local affairs would be administered locally; national governments would be reduced to a concern only with national unity and defense. Finally, since no progress was possible without the development of justice and charity, an attempt would be made to improve the education and the material condition of the masses and to draw them increasingly into a share in all the benefits of society. Lamennais was confident of the support of good men in all nations:

Let the energetic protestations of the human conscience, responding to each other from the banks of the Seine to the heart of Germany, from the plains of Belgium to the seas of Ireland, resound as a single voice, as the purest, most massive cry of liberty the earth has ever heard; yes, something will come from this for the salvation of the world.[20]

* See Appendix A, *14–17*; Appendix B, *3*.

Here was a scope more vast than that of the Agency. Lamennais looked not to France but to the European world. He looked not to the Church in itself, but to the Church as an agent of social renewal. He saw Church liberty as part of a total liberation of mankind. He was involved in yet another effort to find a more perfect basis for society.

Lamennais began to regard the state as virtually unnecessary. He had always distrusted the state, relying primarily on a spiritual power. Now he sought to relegate the government to relatively minor administrative functions.

The new view of the state showed clearly in Lamennais' discussion of the future relationship between Church and secular power. All the editors of the *Avenir* agreed that Church and state should be separated now, as a precondition of the triumph of Catholicism. But once Catholicism had won out, should it then unite with the state and use political as well as religious means? Throughout 1830, all the editors proclaimed that Church and state should by nature be united, that it was only the division of beliefs that necessitated their separation for the present. The new union would be freely formed, by popular demand, but union there would be. Several editors maintained this position throughout the *Avenir's* career; it was, after all, the traditional policy of the Church. Others, such as Lacordaire and Gerbet, paid little attention to future relationships. Lamennais, however, began to alter his views. He felt that human governments should never have any power over men's minds. The use of political means in the spiritual realm would brutalize the noblest features of men. All men were spiritually obliged to believe in Catholicism, but they could never be obliged politically to do so. To be sure, liberty had been justly restricted in the Middle Ages; but then men had been in a state of spiritual infancy. Now, in the Catholic countries, men had grown to maturity under God's guidance. Liberty could and should prevail, then, even after it had united men in the Catholic faith.

The point was that mankind had reached a new stage in its development. Old forms were irrelevant and even criminal. God ruled, of course, as He always had. Neither the will of kings nor the will of the people was sovereign; both had to obey the law of God, or there could be only tyranny. But, since God transmitted sovereignty to governments through the people, it was up to the people to decide what form of government would best realize the divine law. And it was up to the people to change their government whenever it violated divine law.

Here was a decisive change in Lamennais' political views. It coincided with his earlier philosophic contention that God had endowed the general reason of mankind with a certain infallibility. Still, Lamennais had never before been an explicit democrat. At first he fought democracy; toward the end of the Restoration he realized that democracy was inevitable and simply hoped to check it through the restraint of religion; now he ardently advocated it.

There were several important corollaries to Lamennais' democratic politics. First, the people had the right and even the duty to revolt against injustice. Lamennais hailed the revolutions in Poland and Belgium in 1830 as just reactions against a vile tyranny. The *Avenir* also encouraged other people, such as the Irish, in their resistance to oppression. And Lamennais even urged Italy to free itself from Austria. He did adopt a somewhat ambiguous stance when revolution spread to the Papal States, though even here he recommended major political reforms. Finally, Lamennais began to prophesy the doom of the July Monarchy in the same tones he had used during the Restoration. Louis-Philippe was not meeting the needs of the people. He refused to grant universal suffrage, ignored the liberties of the Charter, and persecuted the Church. Resistance to the government was fully justified and outright revolution inevitable.

The institution of monarchy itself, in fact, was doomed to destruction. Lamennais knew that kings could never adhere to the sovereign popular will. A democratic republic was the only suitable form, for it alone could fulfill the law of justice and meet the needs of the time. Lamennais wrote in July 1831: "Seeing all the calamities with which some men burden the world solely in their own interest, I am horrified by everything which is called king."[21]

Government, particularly monarchical government, was worthless; the people were everything. It was therefore the duty of the Church to associate itself with the demands of the masses and help guide them to the greatest possible social good. All Catholics should become the avant-garde of humanity, leading it to the conquest of liberty and the future; and the pope should show the way. Rome should shake off all attachment to human monarchs. But all levels of the Church should participate in the process. Priests, having a special duty to serve as disinterested representatives of the people's needs, should immerse themselves in the desires and hopes of the masses. With this sort of guidance for the movement of humanity, society would be regenerated, and "the last era of human society here below" would be ushered in.[22]

This would be a society in which men would rule themselves, accepting advice from the Church, but voluntarily and without political compulsion. There would be no coercion of the mind. Governments would rule only in general material areas, and even here the people would be free in most spheres. Society would not be perfect, for man would never be fully purified of sin; but it would be more perfect than any system previously conceived. God would be sovereign, but now the untrammeled, spontaneous rule of the people would in effect be the rule of God.

For democracy to prevail fully, one great imbalance had to be corrected. On this matter, Lamennais clearly came under the influence of De Coux; he became a social as well as a liberal Catholic. The division between poor and rich, oppressed and oppressor, had to be radically modified. Lamennais began to talk of the misery and subjection of the working class. Without some alleviation of this misery, rich and poor would war to the death, destroying society. Besides, every man had the right at least to subsist. Lamennais' remedies for misery were rather vague. He talked of the need for generosity and unselfishness. He hoped that priests could stimulate better relations between workers and employers. He urged the government to attend to the needs of the poor. Specifically, he insisted that workers be allowed to associate in their own defense, which was then illegal. Through all these means, but most particularly by spreading a true, Catholic sense of love and charity, the numbers of the poor would be reduced and the problem of poverty made manageable. Here again, a purified Catholicism could join with the people to create the more perfect society.

Lamennais was one of the earliest social Catholics. He knew little about the poor, but he began to sense the existence of new groups of urban workers exploited by capitalist manufacturers. Like most early social Catholics, his proposals were less clear than his concern; they consisted mainly of a traditional sort of charity now greatly extended. But Lamennais brought a passionate sympathy to the impoverished masses unusual for his time and his Church. A strange and one-sided love affair was beginning. Lamennais now went beyond his earlier belief that the people would rule and that the people demanded liberty. He began to develop a sense of special mission to aid and guide the people and to commiserate with their many hardships. He hoped that the Church would follow him in this mission, for the people needed religious solace as well as political and economic reform. But the people were the main goal, the people were the source of all real progress. Lamennais' intense faith in the people is hard to explain. It was a product of the excitement of this revolutionary period, when the people seemed to stand alone against corrupt governments and a misguided Church. The faith was intellectual, abstract; Lamennais had no real contact with the people; but Lamennais' chief passions were always intellectual. Lamennais had gone beyond liberalism. He had developed a loyalty almost unheard of in his day. His isolation doomed him to failure. But his new faith in the people inured him to hardship, for he knew that his faith was well-founded and would triumph.

The doctrines and activities of the *Avenir* had certain confusing implications. To woo Catholics away from legitimism, the paper talked of the need for the Church to free itself from politics altogether. But Lamennais urged Catholicism to guide the democratic and social efforts of the masses. This was a new politics, but quite definitely politics. The paper praised the Revolution of 1830 and its Charter, but all the editors became increasingly disenchanted with the regime; and Lamennais urged or at least predicted revolution. The *Avenir* talked generally in terms of the good of the Church. It was assumed that the advance of the Church would benefit society, but this was not the main emphasis. Correspondingly, the Agency worked for the Church alone. Lamennais, of course, sought to free and support the Church. But for him the Church had to serve society above all; he was not interested in the institution for itself. Lamennais was clearly more radical than his colleagues, and he was also looking at different and broader problems.

There was, however, no open dispute among the editors except on specific matters, for example, how harsh should be the condemnation of the legitimists. Lamennais continued to be publicly revered by all the editors, and his articles were given the central place whenever they appeared. Furthermore, there were real points of unity. All the editors were devoted to advancing Catholicism in and through a liberal system. All hoped to stabilize society on a just basis. To most supporters of the *Avenir*, the editors seemed to be working together to modernize the Church in the interests both of religion and of society.

The differences in orientation were, however, important. They seemed a godsend to many critics of the movement. Lamennais' extravagances could be cited as evidence that liberal Catholicism as a whole was wrong. The idea of eternal separation of Church and state could be ridiculed; in this way the more modest argument that separation was necessary now could be tacitly condemned as well. So it was with most of the major proposals of the *Avenir*.

Ultimately the differences in view were to be important to the editors themselves. While the *Avenir* continued, the excitement and novelty of the project helped mitigate potential disagreement. Montalembert entitled the year 1831 in his diary, "Intoxication of Combat." The editors were all conscious that they were engaged in a vital work, and they loved to do battle for the truth. But as opposition mounted, and particularly when the paper was suspended and there was time for second thoughts, disagreement emerged quickly.

The line of thought Lamennais was now developing was to orient him politically for the rest of his life. He had found a new cause within his persistent interest in seeking a truly orderly basis for society. He was devoted to the people and had confidence in them. Of course the people needed religion; of course the Church should guide them. Lamennais never abandoned a kind of Catholicism. But now he had a clearly independent standard by which to judge the Church. If it allied with monarchical governments, it was not helping the people. If the Church did not help the people, it was wrong. The hand of God was working in the world. The question, as Lamennais saw it in 1831, was whether God was still working in the Church.

CHAPTER V

RESPONSE TO THE *AVENIR*

The *Avenir,* depending heavily on public opinion, sought to rouse both Catholics and liberals. And it had some success. It met, however, with formidable opposition from various sources. This opposition quickly killed the movement. Attacks continued long after the *Avenir* had been abandoned; the bitter hostility to the whole project must be realized. This bitterness gave evidence of the shock that the *Avenir*'s doctrines caused in many circles. It had major repercussions on the editors of the *Avenir,* too.

For Lamennais, the reactions to the *Avenir* were decisive in several respects. The popularity the movement achieved in several quarters convinced him of the validity of his basic approach. He was incapable of a calm, objective evaluation of the support for his doctrines and was constantly open to vast exaggerations of this support. In his excitement, everything he saw pointed to a groundswell of enthusiasm for the *Avenir* on the part of the masses of Catholics and liberals: "Our newspaper is producing a great effect, one which far surpasses what we expected."[1] Yet the steady and mounting opposition revealed the vicious evil present in many ruling groups, in the Church itself. There seemed to be a conspiracy of the powerful against the Mennaisian movement, part of the larger conspiracy of rulers against the people, against the future. The reaction to the *Avenir* set the stage for the final confrontation of Lamennais and the Church.

Support for the *Avenir* came from many parts of France and from abroad. Associations were established under the aegis of the Agency in at least six cities, and others were planned. In Lyons a group collected money for Ireland and undertook legal defense of the right of Catholic procession, on the model of their sponsor. Several local newspapers were founded with the encouragement of the Agency. Papers in Nantes, Nancy, and Strasbourg echoed the doctrines of the *Avenir,* and other provincial papers supported its ideas. Several journals asked the *Avenir* to supply them with editors. The movement did not obtain clear support from every region of France, but it did spread widely.

Outside of France, the widest enthusiasm for the project came, naturally, from Belgium. A number of Belgian papers reprinted *Avenir* articles, and a journal was founded at Liége that published all of them; possibly as many as 4,000 persons subscribed to this paper. And Belgians contributed heavily to the *Avenir's* appeals for funds. Scattered support came from other countries. Several Polish revolutionaries expressed gratitude for the *Avenir's* backing. Articles were reprinted in Germany, and several German liberal Catholics sent occasional essays on the state of religion in their country. The whole Munich liberal Catholic group was enthusiastic, and the philosopher Franz von Baadar wrote a pamphlet in the *Avenir's* defense. The Irish bishops were interested at least in the fund drive in their behalf. The paper received letters from the United States, too. In Holland a newspaper was launched in the image of the *Avenir*. And there was considerable, if less formal, interest in the movement among Italians. The *Avenir* had struck a responsive chord. This was a time of uncertainty all over Europe both for liberalism and for Catholicism. For a significant number of people, among them many prominent thinkers, the *Avenir* provided promising answers to the political problems of the day.

A striking indication of the adherence to the movement occurred in the summer of 1831. The 80,000 francs on which the *Avenir* was founded proved to be inadequate, and this inadequacy was heightened by inefficient management. By May the funds were almost exhausted. Faced with the collapse of their enterprise, the editors appealed for help to all friends of Catholicism and liberty. Additional stocks were put on sale. The editors anxiously waited to learn whether or not they would be able to go on. They were not long in doubt. By September almost all the stocks issued had been sold. Frenchmen contributed 47,000 francs and Belgians 20,500 to keep the project alive.

Over its entire career, the movement collected more than 260,000 francs for its various causes. To be sure, the *Avenir* never had more than 1,500 subscribers at its peak, though some editors later claimed at least 3,000. It did not reach a huge audience. But these were days in which a subscription list of 6,000 was large for a popular paper. Printing costs and taxes kept the price of newspapers high; and the actively literate population was only a minority. Though the circulation of the *Avenir* was tiny, it did not represent failure for a relatively specialized journal. Furthermore, one copy of the paper passed through many hands. In Savoy there were reports that twenty copies regularly circulated among more than a hundred Catholics—despite an edict by the Piedmontese government banning the paper. There is no way to estimate how many people the *Avenir* reached. In France alone it clearly had several thousand supporters. And among these, enthusiasm ran high. Hundreds of letters to the paper told of the excitement caused by liberal Catholic ideas. One priest wrote that he and his friends "walked along with the *Avenir* in our hands, repeating loudly that it should be printed in letters of gold."[2] Again, the movement was not an isolated one. It dealt with problems that were widely felt.

The *Avenir*, seeking to draw on a number of different groups, hoped to appeal to liberals, too. But success here was limited. A few prominent liberals did give their support. The Belgian Potter wrote articles for the *Avenir*, claiming for Catholicism an equal share in the liberties granted to all men. Several radical liberal and republican papers, such as the *Globe*, the *Temps*, and a few provincial journals, generally supported the *Avenir*'s effort to obtain liberty, while maintaining their own non-Catholicism. One paper wrote: "We sincerely defend the rights of our enemies so that we may prove ourselves worthy of demanding these rights in our turn."[3] Several non-Catholic lawyers backed the *Avenir*'s efforts to free the Church on the same basis. A feeling existed that a union was possible in order to attain freedom for all; truth would prevail through liberty. There was no need for agreement now on what the truth was.

Particularly striking was the interest liberal Romantics took in the *Avenir* movement. Literary figures provided the most prominent non-Catholic support for the whole effort. The *Avenir*, by its belief in liberty and in social evolution and by its support of glorious if futile efforts such as the Polish revolution, was distinctly part of the French Romantic current. Because of this affinity, and out of a desire to enlist the support of famous men, the *Avenir* blatantly wooed the Romantics by adopting their views on literature. And both Montalembert and Lamennais had personal contacts with the Romantics that they exploited fully. The results were more than satisfactory. Hugo, Vigny, Lamartine, Balzac, and several other prominent Romantics sent works for the *Avenir* to publish. Hugo and Sainte-Beuve adhered to most of the doctrines of the movement; Sainte-Beuve even temporarily became a Catholic under Lamennais' influence. Lamartine repeated most of the *Avenir*'s ideas in his own political writings of the period—though he remained anxious to give an impression of originality. Chateaubriand showed some favor, and Michelet wrote, "However different our opinions may be, it is impossible not to sympathize with such men."[4]

On February 3, 1831, a banquet was given to celebrate the successful conclusion of the *Avenir's* trial. Victor Hugo was there. Several Protestant lawyers attended. A former editor of the *Globe* represented one liberal faction. It was a joyous occasion, in which doctrinal and personal harmony reigned. The principal toast praised "the definitive union of true Catholicism with true liberalism."[5]

In reality, most liberals opposed the movement. There existed no massive sentiment that Catholicism could safely be freed. Certainly the bulk of the *Avenir's* support did not come from liberal sources. Still, enough individuals did endorse the possibility of a liberal-Catholic union to keep the idea of an alliance alive. This was particularly important for Lamennais, who knew that liberalism was the wave of the future. He claimed that the masses wanted liberty. But he was never concerned with counting the liberals for and against his ideas. It was easy to dismiss liberal opponents as false and backward, to hail friends as representative of the liberalism of the future, the liberalism of the people. The fame of some of his new literary supporters, the sense that they constituted the vanguard of French thought, flattered Lamennais personally and encouraged his belief that he was winning over the type of liberal that really counted. The support won outside France also impressed him. His contacts with Belgium increased; and the liberal-Catholic union was now successful there—it had made a revolution. The proposal for an international union of liberals and Catholics reflected the extent to which Lamennais felt involved now in a world-wide movement. In other words, Lamennais was confirmed in his desire to work for a liberal-Catholic alliance by the support that some, often prominent, liberals gave—however meager and unrepresentative this support seems in retrospect. He began to make some friends among the liberals, to whom he felt both personal and intellectual loyalty; these friendships were to be important later. There seemed no reason to abandon the notion of working with "true" liberals just because some of the old-fashioned suspicion of the Church persisted.

Significantly, Lamennais never expressed great annoyance against the liberals who opposed him. He anticipated this sort of opposition, felt it was unimportant, and even sympathized with its basis, because the Church had so clearly and wrongly alienated liberalism in the past. His tolerance was much greater here than for the Catholics who opposed him. Lamennais' optimism about the purity of liberalism and its ultimate reconcilability with a purified Catholicism increased steadily during the *Avenir's* career.

The most numerous and active support of the *Avenir* was Catholic. It was to Catholics that most of the editors directed their efforts and their lessons. Probably the most ardent backing for the *Avenir* came from small groups of lay Catholic students in Paris and in other university towns. These students loved both Catholicism and liberty, and had been saddened by the apparent conflict between the two. They lived in a hostile, anti-Catholic environment. It was exciting to see a vigorous, modern defense of the Church; it was exciting to seem part of an almost revolutionary movement. How many such students there were cannot be estimated. It is not known how representative they were of Catholic students generally. Clearly, though, their support was enthusiastic and unreserved.

The great bulk of the *Avenir's* support, including over half its subscribers, came from the younger members of the clergy. Young priests and seminarians adhered completely to the *Avenir's* ideas on the proper relationship between

Church and state. They welcomed a defense against government interference in the Church's activities. They backed the concept of accommodation between the Church and the leading political ideas of France. They wanted a more vigorous Church, and the *Avenir* alone seemed to promise this. From young priests came hundreds of letters of praise of the *Avenir*. Most of these expressed intense gratitude that someone was at last rescuing the Church from oppression, as well as a resolution to aid in this effort even at personal sacrifice. Many priests professed willingness to renounce their state salary, and at least one priest did so. A number of priests delivered sermons along the lines of *Avenir* doctrine. The extent of support varied in different dioceses in France, but there was some enthusiasm almost everywhere. Several prelates stated that the whole of the younger clergy was lost to the *Avenir*. This was undoubtedly exaggerated. There is no question, however, that the doctrines of the *Avenir* had won the most vigorous and articulate segment of the young churchmen in France.

Many lay Catholics, other than students, were attracted to the movement also; again, precise numbers cannot be known. A group of laymen in the south wrote: "We saw in your enterprise a work inspired by God, we heard your appeal, we answered it. May all Christians do the same! We believe it is a duty."[6]

Finally, a mood of partial sympathy stretched beyond the actual supporters of the movement. Most of the Catholic press was hostile to the *Avenir*, but only a few papers were totally opposed. Most papers, and presumably many Catholics who shared their views, could be won for specific projects of defense of the Church. Most Catholic papers, therefore, backed the attempt to found a free school and to defend churchmen against government attack. They might disagree with the *Avenir*'s politics or even its larger view of Church-state relations, but they could not fail to support a vigorous defense of the Church. Some even helped sponsor fund-raising drives. There could always be the hope that this partial support could be drawn into a full realization of the benefits of liberty for the Church. Many editors worked for this conversion; the Agency was almost entirely devoted to the sort of specific project that could arouse Catholics of various opinions. Beyond an important nucleus of direct support, then, was a Catholic sentiment of reserve but not total hostility, which could be construed as promising.

Lamennais found the reactions of most Catholics distinctly promising. He was encouraged by the new willingness of many Catholics "to demand the promised liberties by all legal means." He claimed the support of "a great part of the clergy." Again, he exaggerated in all this, but he was honestly convinced that the mass of simple Catholics were behind him or at least potentially so.

In Lamennais' eyes, then, the people were with him, both Catholic and liberal: "Public opinion is for us, and it is fine to defend, in the presence of France, the cause of all Frenchmen."[7] Much of Lamennais' new devotion to the people was based on this sense of a common cause. And this sense also shaped Lamennais' reaction to the new opposition he faced. Opposition did not come from the people; it did not come from true liberals or true Catholics. It had to be an evil plot.

As the Avenir was capable of arousing intense enthusiasm, so it could inspire bitter hatred. The enemies of the movement were not, for the most part, simply indifferent to it or only mildly concerned; they were active. They disagreed violently with the Avenir's position and sought to destroy the movement. They ultimately succeeded.

Most liberals were opposed to liberal Catholicism. Their opposition was not immediately crucial to the movement. They could not influence the Catholics who provided the essential support. And most liberals were not really worried about the *Avenir*. This was one group among which indifference prevailed over active hostility. Still, the *Avenir* did seek the liberals; it is important to note that it largely failed. And the absence of significant liberal interest forced the movement to depend completely on Catholic backing.

Most liberals simply could not believe that Catholics really wanted liberty. Liberal papers recognized that the *Avenir* talked partly in their terms. They supported some useful notions, such as the exclusion of the Church from participation in affairs of state. Many backed the idea of dropping state financial support of the Church, as a means of saving money. It was enjoyable to be able to cite a Catholic paper in defense of such useful, secular proposals. But the idea of uniting with Catholics to free the Church was ridiculous. In the first place, the *Avenir* was not the Church. Liberal papers stressed constantly that liberal Catholicism was a minority movement that the hierarchy could never support. It was fine for Lamennais to urge the abandonment of state pay; but as one paper noted: "Does he believe that his project will please the archbishops, the bishops, and the Catholic priests?"[8] In other words, there was no reason for liberals to modify their view of the Church as a backward, privilege-seeking body, just because of a tiny new movement among Catholics. Consequently most liberals could not accept the idea of freeing the Church from state control. If the government did not keep a firm grip on the Church, Catholics would work to overthrow any liberal regime. To be sure, the Restoration relationship of Church and state had to be changed. But it had to be changed because it was too favorable to the Church, not because it oppressed the Church, as the *Avenir* claimed. And the change should be in the direction of tighter control of the dangerous features of Catholicism.

Most French liberals, then, were not liberal in the *Avenir*

sense. They did not favor a free competition of ideas, Catholic among others, because they were convinced that the
Church would immediately seek dominance. Liberals easily
suspected the *Avenir* movement of being yet another Catholic trick to win privilege. They accused the Agency of attempting to gain control of France on behalf of the Church.
The *Avenir* was denounced for seeking to combine religious
liberty and universal suffrage to create a theocratic political
force that would take over the state. Most commonly, liberals ridiculed the *Avenir's* objections to government action
against the Church. Here was simply another case of the
Church's attempt to rouse Catholics to fanaticism over
harmless state actions and then to use this to overthrow a
revolutionary government. Many liberals, convinced that all
Catholics were irrevocably legitimist, and certainly the
Avenir was Catholic, sincerely suspected the *Avenir* of being
legitimist. The constant criticism of the July Monarchy
could easily confirm the impression that the movement
sought to restore the Bourbons. Wrote one liberal paper:
"While having the appearance of associating with the sentiments which made the revolution, while imperiously demanding the liberty promised by the revolution, the *Avenir*
reveals its secret thought: it is the despotism of the clergy
under Charles X which it regrets; the liberty it wants is the
power to free itself from the laws."[9] Most liberals, content
with the July Monarchy, at least in its early days, were
touchy about the possibility of rightist attack. They knew
the Church was potentially hostile. There seemed no reason
to discern political differences within the Church. The fact
that liberal Catholics refused to accept the religious actions
of the new regime gave clear evidence that the movement
was just a new form of the old Church hostility to liberalism.

Finally, Lamennais was too radical for most French liberals. The talk of universal suffrage and full freedom of the

press raised the threat of lower-class subversion and control. The idea of republicanism was too much to endure. If this was not simply a Catholic trick to restore the Bourbons, then it was dangerous on other grounds. Either way, liberals could agree that the *Avenir* was "an organ of bigotism and civil dissension."[10]

For all its hopes, the *Avenir* did not dent the anti-Church bias of most liberals. It could explain this bias as old-fashioned and unliberal, but it could not remove it. The hostility of liberals was important, even though it did not undermine the whole effort. It encouraged Lamennais to think of going beyond the liberals, to purer, more radical movements, in his effort to unite the Church with modern society. It gave ample argument to Catholics who opposed the *Avenir,* for obviously the talk of liberal-Catholic union was largely nonsense. The liberals would oppose the Church whatever it did; so Catholics should seek all the protection and privilege they could.

The liberal reaction to the *Avenir* revealed the extreme difficulty of founding a durable liberal Catholic movement in France. Such a movement could not expect even vague sympathy from political liberals, save by patient effort and by showing that a substantial segment of the Church was on their side. But conversion of Catholics and even patience itself became difficult while liberal attacks continued. The temptation was either to renounce liberalism and work for the defense of the Church alone or to renounce the Church in the interest of an alliance with the liberal movement.

The French government gave the *Avenir* much the same reception that the liberals did. It was not profoundly concerned, but it was certainly hostile. The government was angered by the continual attacks on the University, the prefects, the appointment of bishops. It had no intention of renouncing control over the Church. It was worried about the possibility of Catholic opposition to the regime and concerned over radical agitation against the regime; the *Avenir* posed a threat on both counts. One civil servant described it as "one of the most anarchistic papers."[11] The prime minister said that the editors worked for the alliance of ultramontane Catholicism with extreme liberal opinion as the basis for new revolution.

The government attempted to hinder the movement in several overt ways. It refused the *Avenir* permission to set up presses in its offices, for these "could serve for the production of works hostile to the institutions of the Revolution of 1830."[12] It seized issues of the paper not only in November 1830 but also during the following March. It urged the Catholic hierarchy to act against the movement, in one case requesting that all Catholic associations be dissolved—an obvious reference to the Agency. And always it watched the movement. The police checked the travels of the editors. Prefects often tried to discourage residents of their areas from contributing to charities or signing petitions backed by the movement. In one instance a prefect sent agents to all local citizens who had received an Agency prospectus, to tell them that the Agency was devoted to the Bourbon cause. In August a court fined the paper 3,000 francs for having falsely accused a mayor of persecuting Catholics; during the hearings the judge called the *Avenir* a "fanatical newspaper."[13] Finally, the foreign ministry was active, later on, in pressing the papacy for a condemnation of the whole movement.

The French government was not alone in its fear of the *Avenir*. Piedmont banned the paper, and Austria and probably Russia and Prussia took diplomatic steps against it in Rome. These governments were concerned both with the movement's support for revolutions in Poland and Belgium and with the idea of an international union of liberals and Catholics.

The opposition of governments, like that of liberals,

helped orient the later doctrines of the *Avenir* and, particularly, those of Lamennais himself. It showed that existing regimes were rotten. It showed that the French government, for all its revolutionary air, was just as bad as the old-regime states of the rest of Europe. It showed that all kings were evil. This explained the official policies, but it did not remove them. The repressive acts of the French government were not terribly damaging. They bothered the movement locally and they certainly posed financial burdens through the fines the courts levied. But there was no full attack. Far more important, in the long run, was the pressure on the papacy. Metternich helped prepare the ultimate condemnation of the whole movement. The *Avenir* was significant enough to rouse the opposition of the established order. It was not powerful enough to meet this opposition.

The most crucial and bitter resistance to the *Avenir* came from the Church itself. Even government repression worked primarily through the Church. Here was the point on which the movement was particularly vulnerable. It depended on financial backing from Catholics. Its doctrinal position was based on a claim to Catholicity. Yet it did not win the Church. From the first, the movement encountered Catholic opposition, which gradually grew, took many forms, and eventually became so overwhelming that the *Avenir* perished.

There was mild resistance to the movement from some liberal Catholics. The *Avenir* put moderate liberal Catholics in a real dilemma. They, too, wanted to reconcile Catholicism with modern society. They, too, wanted liberty for the Church and for all men. But they were not radical. They wanted to dissociate the Church from political causes, but they did not want full separation of Church and state. They wanted freedom for truth, but they did not admit that error had any right to such freedom. Many of them were royalists, and looked more to the supporters of the Bourbons than to the liberals for aid in the defense of the Church. All were opposed to the democratic leanings of the *Avenir*. Many of these people were friends of the *Avenir* editors. All supported many aspects of the movement. But they could not accept the whole of it. Several efforts, led by Montalembert, to unite these men with the *Avenir* failed; Lamennais and most of his colleagues regarded the moderates as impossibly indecisive. As a result, the moderate movement went into eclipse. It could not withstand the competition of the more vigorous and persuasive *Avenir*.

The opposition of the moderates was not really important. Few of them objected to the *Avenir* publicly; they just withheld support. Their position is worth noting, however. If the *Avenir* was too radical for men who supported freedom and modernity, what could it be for the bulk of the Church? The moderates had the only approach that could have worked within the French Church, because they respected tradition and urged only gradual and partial change. The *Avenir* hurt their cause. Few opponents of the *Avenir* would distinguish between the liberty it discussed and that which moderate liberal Catholics urged; it was easy to condemn the whole idea of change. The alienation of the moderates did far more than deprive the *Avenir* of a bit more support; it ultimately weakened the whole liberal movement in the Church.

The vital and direct resistance to the movement came, of course, from the Church hierarchy, the older clergy, and the many conservative laymen attached to the Church. These people were resolutely opposed to any change in the Church. As the *Avenir* urged change on many fronts, the conservatives raised many serious objections to the movement.

The French hierarchy, still firmly Gallican, automatically opposed any project in which Lamennais was involved, because of his earlier ultramontanism. And it was antagonized by the ultramontanism the *Avenir* professed. This was not their main objection to the movement, and there was no direct criticism now of ultramontanism itself. The hierarchy looked to papal support against liberal Catholicism, so it refrained from attacking papal power. And bishops could no longer rely so firmly on government sympathy. To this extent there was an interesting change from the Restoration period. Still, the Gallican tradition was strong and the *Avenir* was denounced for its harshness to the tradition, which was held to be a legitimate opinion.

Related to continued Gallicanism was the persistent belief in the need for Church-state union. The *Avenir's* desire for separation of Church and state was vigorously resisted. Few Catholics could see that the Church's situation was so bad that such radical measures were necessary. They were anxious not to antagonize the government by complaining too much about its treatment of the Church. Further, few French Catholics could conceive of separation from the state. The Church had a duty to support stable government, and the state's help was certainly vital for the Church, especially in an age of popular anti-Catholicism. It was easy to recall the period of the great revolution, when the Church had been cut off from the state and driven into hiding; surely the experiment did not bear repetition. The Church should press for as much restriction of error as possible. To be sure, the Church could use more freedom in teaching and association, but to grant these liberties generally would encourage impiety rather than religion. The state budget was essential, too. Without it, the Church would be reduced to degrading appeals to the charity of the faithful; and in an age of widespread atheism, there was no guarantee that enough money would be obtained. The status quo was not ideal, but it was better than any other possible arrangement.

Here was the crucial difference between the *Avenir* and the majority of Catholics. Both sides agreed that the state was not always beneficial to the Church. Both sides agreed that there was a massive problem of popular irreligion. But where the *Avenir* saw a solution only in a daring liberal experiment, the bulk of the Church felt that reliance on the state was more vital than ever. The indignities the government fostered could be endured with Christian resignation. If it were really a choice between slavery and freedom, obviously the Church should abandon the state; but this was not the case. The key point was to use the existing system to best advantage, not to challenge it. One of the leading opponents of Lamennais wrote: "Let your devotion be governed by prudence. Attach yourself more than ever to the traditions received from the fathers in the faith."[14] The ideas of the *Avenir* were not only impractical; they were subversive.

The Church leaders rejected out of hand the purely political ideas of the movement. Whether Catholics were partisans of the Bourbons or of the July Monarchy, they were alienated by the radicalism of the *Avenir*. The democratic ideas of the movement were condemned as detrimental both to political stability and to the sovereignty of God. The idea of supporting just revolutions seemed absurd, particularly when the whole revolutionary movement was so clearly hostile to Catholicism. To most Catholics, a revolution was never just; the Christian's duty was submission even to the most tyrannical government, for the sake of order in society. The notion of a union with liberalism, finally, was extremely dangerous. What good could come of an alliance with the worst enemies of God and government? "What society is there between light and shadows, what agreement between Christ and Belial, what relationship between the faithful and the unfaithful?"[15], wrote a conservative Belgian priest. The unalterable hostility of most liberals was matched by the inflexible hatred of most Catholics.

The leading elements of the French Church rejected the religious and political ideas of the *Avenir*. Both involved radical novelty, so both were condemned. There was a final source of dispute as well, and not the least important. To the older clergy and especially to the bishops, the whole methodology of the movement was rank insubordination. Here were simple priests and laymen acting on their own, without the permission of their ecclesiastical superiors, discussing matters and doing things that should never be discussed or done without prior approval of the hierarchy. This had long been an objection to Lamennais' approach; but now this approach was extended to hundreds, perhaps thousands, of other Catholics as well. Priests and laymen were being urged to copy the independent actions of the leaders of the movement. Organizations of Catholics were formed without any permission from above. There was real fear that the use of modern journalism and especially the formation of a national league of Catholics directed by priests was an attempt to usurp control of the Church, to "subject the whole Church to their dictatorship."[16] These were simply not the proper sources of guidance in the Church, and the hierarchical tradition was extremely strong. One of the real gains of French bishops through the Concordat had been the increase of their local power. The *Avenir* movement was undermining one of the foundations of order in the Church.

The basic objections to the Mennaisian movement were presented forcefully and frequently during 1830 and 1831. Catholic newspapers, both local and national, attacked all the liberal Catholic doctrines. A number of pamphlets were prepared, some under direct episcopal sponsorship. The *Avenir* tried to counter all the arguments, but it could not stem the flood of attack. The movement became a major issue in the French Catholic press.

Public arguments were not, however, the principal feature of the campaign against the *Avenir*. There were reasoned discussions of the issues, but there was outright slander as well. Catholic papers such as the *Ami de la Religion* distorted isolated phrases from the *Avenir* and even invented complete falsehoods to embarrass their opponents. In Lamennais' trial, for example, his lawyer had called him the regenerator of Catholicism. It was shocking enough to use a Protestant lawyer, but this phrase was even worse. If Catholicism needed a regenerator, it was therefore now degenerate —and this proved that Lamennais was aiding the opponents of the Church, who also called Catholicism degenerate. Repeated protests by Lamennais that he did not agree with this did not stop the slander. Beyond this, wild stories were spread throughout France. Reports were published about revolutionary conspirators who joined the editors of the *Avenir* in plotting disturbances of the peace. A letter was invented purporting to come from Lamennais, urging priests to unite to destroy the episcopate; it was circulated among the southern French clergy. In this case Lamennais was able to trace the author of the letter and to obtain a public apology from him. However, other rumors were spread so secretly that there was no opportunity to rectify them; they did untold harm to the *Avenir's* cause among clergy and faithful. No holds were barred in the effort to divert support from the movement.

The campaign against Lamennais was by no means new, but never had it reached such a peak. The man seemed subversive of all the disciplinary, political, and even theological traditions of the Church. The whole force of Catholic hatred of innovation was directed against him. Hence the bitterness and nastiness of the effort. It was easy for Lamennais to see the injustice of this virtual persecution within the French Church. He was saddened by it, more often deeply angered by it, and progressively was driven to rethink his relationship to the Church.

Here is an irony. Lamennais' opponents used nasty methods and unfair arguments; yet they were often right. They sensed in Lamennais something that Lamennais did not fully realize of himself: there were no clear limits to the innovations that Lamennais sought. The battle was not simply between bigoted reactionaries and a noble defender of the best interests of the Church. Lamennais was sure he was acting in the Church's best interests, but he was equally sure that he was the final judge of these interests; he would brook no argument. And increasingly, he began to contemplate changes in the form of the Church itself, in the interests of true religion and a better society. Unlike almost all his associates, he was not committed to the Church above all; he had his overrriding vision of God and society. Hence his Catholic critics and slanderers were often right or at least prophetic. It was nasty to claim that Lamennais had talked of a regeneration of Catholicism; it was untrue, as of early 1831; but within a year, though only privately, Lamennais was convinced that a regeneration was precisely what was necessary.

In fact, during 1831, a gap was opening between Lamennais' public and private pronouncements. This was not due to hypocrisy. It was due to the real tensions that Lamennais was feeling between his commitment to social reform and his devotion to the Church. Periodically for the next three years Lamennais protested his orthodoxy. But his orthodoxy often wavered in private. He increasingly realized the hostility between real Catholicism and the democratic Catholicism of which he dreamed; but he could not abandon his dream. He was appalled by the means his opponents used: "intrigues, interdicts, silent plots . . . a terrible system of calumnies."[17] Opponents of this sort could not be truly Christian; there was deep evil within the Church itself. Yet he did not abandon the Church. He protested his obedience virtuously and often, and he was shocked and confused that his opponents would not take him at his word.

The greatest specific villain within the Church, as Lamennais saw it, was the episcopacy, and certainly the hostility of the bishops caused the greatest damage to the *Avenir*. The bishops had long opposed Lamennais' philosophy and his ultramontanism; they were vociferously hostile to his new project. They began in 1831 to manifest their opposition. Many forbade the priests of their dioceses to read the *Avenir*. They fired seminary professors suspected of liberalism and prevented liberal graduates of the seminaries from entering the priesthood. Conciliatory bishops warned Lamennais privately that he should abjure his new doctrines, that the episcopate was against him. Other bishops began to condemn the movement publicly, at least by implication. They were somewhat hesitant at first, perhaps because they feared the strength of the *Avenir*'s support. But in their Lenten letters of 1831 several bishops warned their charges against "profane novelties," no matter how seductive they might appear.[18] One bishop directly condemned the idea of renouncing the state budget and spoke against the general spirit of independence that the *Avenir* represented. Cardinal Rohan addressed a letter from Rome to his diocese, denouncing the new ideas and implying that the Holy See also disapproved. In August the Archbishop of Toulouse warned against "these bizarre systems and absurd errors,"[19] and soon other bishops specifically ordered their clergy to stick to the old doctrines. Finally, later in 1831, the Archbishop of Toulouse drew up a formal condemnation; it was ultimately signed by almost all the bishops of France. It dealt largely with Lamennais' philosophical ideas, but also condemned the advocacy of any change in the Church, disapproval of the Concordat and the relationship with the state, freedom of the press and liberty for error in any form, the right of revolution, and the idea that Gallican doctrines were necessarily erroneous.

Lamennais had never thought highly of the French bishops, but he was disturbed by their new vehemence and blindness to the truth. He tried, publicly, to set to rest the

notion that he was insubmissive to the episcopacy. He wrote
to the vicar general of Marseilles, asserting his "respect for
the episcopacy . . . a submission limited only by what is
owed above all to the sovereign pontiff. This is my profession of faith and I hope to remain faithful to it until my
dying breath."[20] But privately, he was extremely bitter.

The higher clergy is precipitating Religion into the stupid and
infamous intrigues [of the royalists]. . . . The bishops killed
everything: they are forbidding people to read our journal; they
are persecuting priests suspected of attachment to our doctrines;
they are moving heaven and earth to revive Gallicanism, thus
atttracting a hatred against the Church whose consequences
frighten me. . . . Victory would have been certain, and never
would the Church have been stronger or freer. But no: its
leaders have said it must die, it must. . . . I will stop.[21]

In fact, the *Avenir* movement had been killed by the resistance of the French Church. The only hope was that somehow the leaders of that Church could be circumvented.

The editors of the *Avenir* tried to counter the attacks of
the French Church, but the situation was discouraging.
They were ready to quit in May, but the success of their
appeal for funds revived their enthusiasm. By October,
however, the situation seemed impossible once more. The
paper was again in serious financial trouble. The cost of the
trials and the heavy daily expenses of the paper threatened
to overwhelm the enterprise. The increasing opposition of
the bishops, which often endangered the security and position of adherents to the movement, progressively reduced
the number of the paper's subscribers. By October more
than one hundred subscribers had withdrawn, sometimes
with great reluctance. This reduced the earnings of the
paper and seemed to undermine the whole future of liberal
Catholicism in France. Hate and calumny were rising
everywhere. The enemies could not be stilled. The only recourse was to withdraw from active combat. As Lacordaire

put it, "Silence today is the only strength of our cause. It is time for our work to be calmly observed while we ourselves are no longer visible in it."[22] By November the editors had decided to give up. They hoped that their ideas would germinate and eventually conquer the adversary forces.

Still, there was one avenue that had yet to be tested. Lamennais and his colleagues had long professed total obedience to the papacy. The pope had not pronounced on their movement. One of the most devastating arguments bishops and publicists used against the movement stated that Rome could not possibly support such radicalism in the Church. Among the many rumors circulated were reports that the pope had spoken out against Lamennais. But the situation was not clear. Because of their own ultramontane loyalties, the editors needed to straighten out their relations with the pope.

In fact, the pope had not spoken. There were many reasons why he would not do so. Why should Rome undermine a movement that was trying to defend the Church, often with some success? Why should it attack men who professed far clearer loyalty to the papacy than did most of their French opponents? Why should it disavow one of the intellectual giants of Catholicism? There were certainly many reasons not to approve the movement, but why speak at all? There was no sign that the movement was winning overwhelming support. Silence would hardly encourage further support, yet it would leave untouched the ideas that held promise.

Pressure for a pronouncement was building up in 1831. French émigrés in Rome, including Cardinal Rohan and many Jesuits, worked arduously to obtain a condemnation. They had a long-standing hatred of Lamennais and detested his new doctrines as well. From these men came the first statements that the pope disapproved of the liberal movement.

Several papal nuncios sent excited reports to Rome concerning the *Avenir*. The nuncio in Paris stressed the unauthorized character of the movement and the confusion it was injecting into French Catholicism. He also warned that the *Avenir* was really working for the dissolution of society. A former nuncio in Piedmont termed Lamennais "one of the greatest enemies of the Church."[23] Reports of these views were published, adding to the impression that Rome was hostile.

There was other opposition in Rome. Several churchmen close to the pope, one of them a friend of Lamennais, published formal criticisms of the *Avenir*'s doctrines. Still there was no direct word from the pope himself.

In this situation, the editors themselves precipitated the matter. They decided to go to Rome.

The *Avenir* had long sought to counter the reports of papal disapproval. The editors were particularly shocked at rumors that Lamennais would not yield even to a papal pronouncement. Time and time again the paper had professed complete obedience to Rome. Early in 1831 Gerbet drew up a declaration of the principal doctrines for submission to papal judgment; the editors promised to bow to the verdict, whatever it might be.* However, they were unable to send this document to Rome. The papal nuncio refused to transmit it, and the French government, to which the editors appealed, accepted the mission but did not carry it out. The editors long assumed that Rome was for some reason taking no action, so they still felt justified in claiming that silence was an indication of approval. And there were leading churchmen in Rome who wrote that the pope did agree with the main ideas. The confusion persisted.

When the *Avenir* had to cease publication, by November 1831, Lacordaire proposed that a new effort be made to obtain papal judgment. Rather than stopping altogether, why

* See Appendix A, *18–19.*

not simply suspend the paper and go to Rome to see the pope?

The idea had many merits. Even a condemnation would be better than a spineless surrender to the vile opponents in France. And if approval was obtained, as the editors expected, the effort could be resumed with every chance of success. The liberals would see that the *Avenir* really did represent the Church. The French bishops and their allies would be overridden. Supporters of the movement could continue without any fear of being unorthodox. The editors themselves would be relieved of doubts concerning their position. Lacordaire and others had been troubled by the wave of attack on liberal Catholicism; they needed to know what Rome thought.

Lamennais granted the validity of all these arguments. But his own view of the papacy had been changing; here was another vital aspect of his ambiguity toward the Church. He went to Rome with intentions that differed from those of his colleagues. He had long realized, and had written privately, that the pope almost certainly did not approve of the *Avenir*'s political views. He bitterly condemned, though still privately, papal alliance with such governments as the Hapsburg monarchy. He was appalled by the politics of repression practiced in the Papal States. And he had little respect for the new pope, Gregory XVI. Why, then, did he go to Rome?

There were several reasons. In the first place, Lamennais had to get out of France. Deeply in debt, in the autumn of 1831 he was ordered to repay or be arrested. Hostile newspapers attributed his taking the trip to a desire to avoid jail. This is nonsense. Lamennais always acted primarily from principle. Still, his personal difficulties may have been a factor in his decision.

More important, Lamennais saw the trip as a last chance to persuade the pope to adopt liberal views. His whole position, long before the *Avenir* project, had been based on the idea of papal leadership in the world. Now that the pope was expected to guide the liberation of humanity, it was vital to convince the papacy to see the true interests of the Church and accept a Catholic regeneration of society. Rome was currently in league with its worst enemies, against its own doctrines and defenders. But surely it could be reformed. Lamennais' ultramontane faith was shaken, but not destroyed. Rome was on the wrong path, but it could and had to be corrected.

Finally, Lamennais did not intend to submit his political doctrines for direct papal judgment. For several months he had been developing the idea that the pope had no right to rule upon the political ideas of Catholics. The pope had control only over the doctrines and discipline of the Church. Here he was infallible, and here Lamennais was still confident of complete papal approval. Lamennais went to Rome convinced, then, that condemnation was impossible. There was no question of the *Avenir's* religious orthodoxy. Its efforts were clearly in the interests of the Church. As to politics, where Lamennais had new reservations about papal authority, Rome would come around eventually; a visit might speed the conversion. And there was no danger of condemnation on this score, because Lamennais no longer gave the pope authority in politics. It might be illogical to seek ultimate papal guidance for the political liberation of mankind and still deny the pope political power at the present, but such was Lamennais' thinking. Going to Rome convinced that he was right, he did not feel a personal need for papal judgment. But he did see the utility of such a judgment, and was sure he could obtain a correct one.*

On November 15 the last issue of the *Avenir* informed the public that Lamennais, Lacordaire, and Montalembert were going to Rome to seek the verdict of the papacy on their

* See Appendix A, 19–20.

work.* Until judgment was rendered, the *Avenir* would be suspended. If the verdict was unfavorable, the editors promised submission; but if it was favorable, the paper would be resumed immediately. And the Agency would continue while the verdict was being sought.

The editors set out with high hopes. They were taking the only alternative to the complete abandonment of their vital work. They were also taking the first step toward precipitating ultimate papal condemnation of their movement. The final stage of Lamennais' relation with the Church was under way. The gulf between the Church and liberty was about to be widened.

* See Appendix B, 4.

CHAPTER VI

LAMENNAIS AND GREGORY XVI

Three years elapsed between the suspension of the *Avenir* and the complete breakup of the movement. The frenetic activity of 1830–1831 gave way to years of negotiation and definition. Each side probed the other, in the process drifting into greater rigidity. And this was not an abstract exercise; these were years of agonizing personal drama for the major participants.

The many events after the suspension centered around two basic questions. First, how would Rome act? There was little doubt that the papacy could not approve the doctrines of liberal Catholicism, but would it actually disapprove? Would it treat Lamennais with care, seek to win him over, or conciliate him and leave some issues in doubt? Second, how would Lamennais and his colleagues react to the papal position? Almost inevitably they would be forced to choose to some degree between their social and political program and their attachment to the Church. For some of the participants this was not a new choice. Lacordaire and Montalembert had, as young men, faced the dilemma during the Restoration, for they had found their ideas on liberty in apparent conflict with their love of the Church. At that time they had, with reluctance, chosen the Church over liberty. Now they faced a similar problem, though in a much more public arena; and they ultimately made the same decision. For Lamennais and some of his closer disciples the choice was a new one. Lamennais had always assumed an intimate connection between Church and society. He had seen frequently that sections of the Church were following incorrect policies but had never regarded the errors as permanent. Fundamentally, he had always attributed to the Church, at least to Rome, the role that he felt socially necessary at the time. Since his primary concern was always with society, when the Church seemed to have come into definitive conflict with society, there was no longer any real reason for remaining in the Church.

The first question, what the Church would do, dominated the year following the suspension of the *Avenir*. Lamennais devoted himself primarily to the attempt to obtain a verdict. His stay in Rome changed his views on the papacy, but this was not the major development of the year. By the end of 1832 the Church's position was clear. There remained problems of tactics, of how to handle Lamennais. But now the principal issue rested with Lamennais himself: how would he react to the Church's pronouncement? Again, his response seems almost inevitable. The break with the Church was not easy. Lamennais' whole adult life had been spent in the Church, and Catholicism had long been intellectually essential to him. He had to make choices both in principles and in emotions. The intellectual break was easiest, as Lamennais' system of thought scarcely needed the Church. But the emotional ties were strong. They linked Lamennais not so much to the institution but to the only friends he had—to his disciples and colleagues, even to his brother. And Lamennais depended greatly on friendship.

Lamennais was almost alone in choosing the course he did; all of his collaborators eventually adhered to the Church. Even Lamennais did not act quickly, and he long claimed that he had not broken completely. Yet he did

break. He renounced his past, his profession, his friends. By
1834 he had decided to act on principle, no matter what the
cost. His decision was courageous; it was the only one consistent with Lamennais' character.

Lamennais' actions in the years 1832–1834 definitely
widened the breach between liberalism and Catholicism, in
France and elsewhere. Lamennais did not really force new
Church policies, but he did cause the public enunciation of
the policies. Much that could have been left unsaid or
ambiguous had to be defined because of the controversy
with Lamennais. Liberal Catholicism, although not dead,
was now a marginal movement. In France the triumph of
Lamennais' enemies made a real current of reform in the
Church virtually impossible. These were years of failure for
Lamennais. He could not remake the Church; he abandoned
it to what he assumed would be its imminent destruction.
But even in failure, Lamennais retained power. He could
force his opponents into statements of principle that seemed
fully as rigid as his own.

Lamennais and his two colleagues arrived in Rome at the
worst possible moment. Gregory XVI was new to his office
and unsure of his position. He had been a Benedictine monk,
with little experience of the world. He had scarcely been out
of the monastery until he was made cardinal. The new pope
was untrained in politics and deeply conservative. He felt
that the princes of Europe were representatives of God, to
be supported without fail unless the highest interests of the
Church were involved. He feared revolution. In 1832 he
condemned the Polish revolt against Russia, though it was a
rising of Catholics against non-Catholic repression; for in
this chaotic age it was impossible to countenance resistance
to the established order. He recognized the Belgian revolution, again a case of Catholics against non-Catholics, only in
1842. This was the man to whom Lamennais proposed the

alliance of Church and people against the tyranny of kings.

Gregory had, moreover, acceded to the papacy in the midst of a bitter insurrection in the Papal States. This experience obviously colored his political views. He countenanced the savage repression that his leading cardinals urged. Special commissions were established to issue summary trials to the revolutionaries. And the repression was in full swing in 1831, when Lamennais reached Rome. In the midst of fighting the revolts, the pope could hardly sympathize with a radical version of liberal Catholicism. Even though the doctrines involved were important, Gregory was too distracted by more immediate problems to pay much attention to a simple French priest.

In this situation pressures from the outside greatly influenced the papal attitude toward Lamennais. The French bishops, continuing their campaign, in the spring of 1832 submitted their condemnation of Mennaisian doctrines for papal approval. They insisted vigorously and often that Lamennais must not be sent home with anything less than formal papal censure. Representatives of the French government and of others urged the pope to speak out. Of crucial importance was the activity of Metternich and his ambassador to Rome. Metternich sent the pope long letters blasting Lamennais' doctrines. He spoke of the possible dissolution of society due to the exaltation of unruly minds, particularly in France. He noted that it was his duty to go beyond the usual limits of his secular authority to warn the Holy See of the danger both to society and to religion that Lamennais represented. These arguments, presented frequently, put important pressure on the pope. They coincided with Gregory's own vague political views; they came from the chief minister of the leading legitimate monarchy in Europe. And they came from a state on which the papacy depended for the preservation of order in Italy. Metternich did not content himself with arguments; from time to time he transmitted secret reports on Lamennais' attitudes and activities; he even sent personal letters that his agents had seized.

Lamennais was faced, then, with a conservative pope, fearful of revolutionary agitation at home and pressed by insistent Catholic and secular leaders that strong action was necessary. Many of the principal figures in the papal court were hostile to Lamennais, though there were a few supporters; and Gregory depended heavily on advisers in such matters. The conservative forces of Europe had drawn together against the revolutionary dangers evident since 1830. With most Church leaders opposed to any change, the Church was part of European conservatism. The pope was a conservative monarch in his own states. Since the liberal movement was evil in itself, liberalism within the Church was unthinkable.

The pope did not, however, move quickly to condemn Lamennais; nor did he initially intend to condemn him at all. When Lamennais arrived in Rome, the pope was scarcely aware of his new doctrines. There had been no chance to examine the *Avenir*'s ideas. No one, either for or against the movement, had presented the ideas for examination; and there had been more pressing matters to attend to. Clearly, from the frequent complaints of the French bishops, a question of lack of discipline was involved. There seemed no reason to question Lamennais' orthodoxy yet; there is some evidence that the pope did not consider the liberal Catholic doctrines particularly important at this time. Gregory, a fair man, recognized Lamennais' great service to the Church and to the papacy in the past. He realized that the measures Lamennais' enemies demanded were unduly severe. Most of all, perhaps, the pope wanted to avoid the bother of engaging in direct controversy. One of the strengths of the Church had always been its ability to avoid coming to prematurely rigorous decisions. At this time, especially, when the Church was under attack from so many sources, dispute should be avoided. It was best to let the matter drop. A long silence would humiliate Lamennais and return him to proper discipline within the Church. It would punish him for having raised needless trouble. And it would dodge the embarrassing problem of a doctrinal decision.

Despite the many motives for direct condemnation of liberal Catholicism, there was no immediate desire to pronounce. For all his dependence on the Hapsburg monarchy, the pope was reluctant to yield to Metternich's interference in Church affairs. The desire to support the French bishops did not obscure the fact that many of these same bishops usually resisted papal authority. So there was good reason to temporize. It was clear that if a pronouncement was made, it would be unfavorable to Lamennais; the position of the pope required this. But it was not clear that a pronouncement was necessary. Ironically the papal policy of silence defeated itself. The silence aroused Lamennais, and it was Lamennais who precipitated the statement from Rome

The trip to Rome was exasperating to Lamennais; traveling tired him dreadfully. Even on the way to Rome he had argued with Lacordaire over what to do if the pope condemned their movement. Lacordaire advocated complete submission, but Lamennais refused to commit himself. In Rome Lamennais encountered a deliberately cold reception, contrasting vividly with the warmth of his welcome during his earlier trip in 1824. It left little hope for a favorable verdict. Furthermore, there were depressing signs of papal politics in Italy. On his way to Rome Lamennais saw chained bands of political prisoners. In Rome he was shocked at the high-handed repression the papal administration practiced. And then there was the eternal waiting, amid the intrigues against him and in a city he hated. Lamennais' mood became increasingly black.

Soon after their arrival the editors drew up a new statement of principles to submit to the papacy. Two months elapsed before they had any reply. Then, in February 1832, a cardinal wrote to them criticizing polemics in the Church and giving them permission to return to France while their doctrines were being examined. It was an obvious hint that the pope disapproved of their efforts but wished to avoid any formal judgment. Lacordaire understood. He returned to France and kept silent. Lamennais felt that a definite decision was vital. He could not return to France anyway, for his legal problems were not cleared up yet. And he could not endure the ambiguous state in which the pope wished to leave matters. He insisted on an audience. On March 1 he saw Gregory. But he was not allowed to discuss substantive issues, and he found the pope cold and banal. They exchanged a few trite phrases; the pope gave him some trinkets. This was the reward for the great defender of Catholicism and the papacy. Lamennais' bitterness deepened.

By the spring the mission was obviously a failure. Lamennais was not going to obtain a favorable pronouncement. He was not able to convert anyone to his doctrines, for almost no one would receive him. At the same time, the pope had failed with Lamennais. He had not understood that Lamennais required careful treatment. He had not tried to win him personally or to use his prestige to persuade Lamennais to abandon his position. Lamennais could be swayed by emotion as well as principle. In Rome he was left with principle alone.

Lamennais was certain that he understood the papal policies.* He knew well the political pressures being applied in his case. He believed that Rome was hopelessly corrupt. The pope himself was a good monk, but naïve and powerless. Since the real power came from the crowned heads of Eu-

* See Appendix A, 20–23.

rope, there was no use relying on Rome any further. At the same time, Lamennais remained sure that Rome would never condemn him. He was encouraged in this by some ill-advised but highly placed friends in Rome, including one cardinal. He still felt convinced of the absolute orthodoxy of his position; he knew the true interests of the Church. And he was bored. He longed to return to the fight for his cause. Late in July he and Montalembert left Rome, "this great tomb where one finds only bones."[1] He stated publicly that he intended to resume the *Avenir*. Papal silence to him meant tacit approval; public approval was prevented only because of the intrigues against him. Lamennais meant what he said and made some preliminary arrangements to resume publication in Paris. On the way home, in Munich, he met with Lacordaire and enlisted his tentative support for a new effort. Lamennais was going to become active again.

This was more than the papacy could tolerate. Gregory felt that he had treated Lamennais with great forbearance. His silence was only tactical; his basic position on the doctrines of liberal Catholicism could only be hostile. He might resist pressures of bishops and governments for a formal pronouncement, but he could never allow a resumption of the Mennaisian movement. Gregory finally issued a condemnation. He avoided direct mention of Lamennais or the *Avenir;* he still hoped to allow a chance for face-saving, for he did not want to drive Lamennais out of the Church. But the condemnation was clear and sweeping.

The encyclical *Mirari vos** formally condemned the leading ideas of the *Avenir*. It condemned the notion that the Church needed regeneration; that Church and state should be separate; that liberty of the press and liberty for error were desirable; that just revolutions were possible; that associations could be formed between Catholics and non-Catholics; and that any act in the Church could be under-

* See Appendix C, 1.

taken without the approval of the bishops. It gave the princes of Europe a specific role as defenders of the Church. It bitterly lamented the evils of the modern world. The encyclical upheld the political traditions of the Church. The pope insisted on the maintenance of full hierarchical control within the Church, which guaranteed the perpetuation of conservative policies; no impetus could come from below. The policies on which a union with liberal forces could be based were specifically renounced. The Church associated itself fully with political conservatism.

Lamennais received the encyclical while he was in Munich. With the advice of Lacordaire and Montalembert, he decided upon submission. On September 10 the *Avenir* and the Agency were publicly dissolved. Most of the local papers and associations that had followed the direction of the *Avenir* also ceased. Everywhere clerical and lay adherents of the movement made public retractions. Lamennais avoided any public renunciation of his views, but his docility and obedience seemed manifest.*

Most of the liberal Catholics in France submitted in spirit as well as in form. Lacordaire, for example, did not surrender his love for liberty, but he radically modified it to correspond to the expressed will of the Holy See. He, and many others like him, resolved to engage in Catholic activities that would remove him from the dangers of political action. This was not the case with Lamennais, who abandoned his works because the pope had disapproved but did not abandon the ideas the pope had condemned. He went back to Brittany and seemed to devote himself to his teaching; he recruited a number of new students for his effort to modernize the intellectual basis of Catholicism. For weeks he might appear satisfied with his studies, his lessons, and the peace and quiet of La Chesnaie. But his soul was troubled. He took no pleasure in his apparent loyalty to the pope; rather, he saw

* See Appendix A.

this as a violation of true Christianity. In December 1832 Lacordaire broke with him definitively, because of the rebelliousness that Lamennais felt free to express in private. This was the first full defection, but it was not the last. Many former associates were compelled to renounce Lamennais, often following this with elaborate condemnations of their former master. The process was not a pretty one. It is galling to see men denounce their past and revile their former leader. The successive rejections reflected the continuing battle between Lamennais and the French Church. Lamennais did not repent.* He did not even seek to bend his doctrines to fit the papal edict, while continuing his efforts as best he could. He was busily developing new ideas to explain the action of the pope and to leave himself free to continue his work for society outside the Church. For its part, the French Church, not content to leave him alone, was resolved to reduce him to humble obedience or to drive him out.

Even in Rome Lamennais had been evolving a new theory of the Church. He had long talked of the need to regenerate society under the guidance of Catholicism. Now he added a belief in the necessary regeneration of the Church. He did not pretend that man would effect this regeneration; God would do so. God would remake the Church in a manner appropriate to the society of the future. Just as Christ had brought a new religion to raise mankind above barbarism, so Catholicism would be replaced to suit the new stage of human development. The papacy was hopeless; as it could not lead, it had to be outwaited. Only God remained constant. All hope was in God and in the people whom God had raised to leadership in society.

Kings were still evil and the poor still had to be freed from their oppressors. Lamennais' political and economic views remained unchanged from those of the later *Avenir* period;

* See Appendix A, 25–29.

they had simply become firmer. His realization that the whole Church had to be altered as part of the general social change was new. It was no longer a question of reforms; it was no longer a question of citing older Catholic authorities as the basis for criticism of current policies. With the pope's betrayal of true religion, Lamennais lost all hope of change within the Church. There was no abandonment of religion itself. Lamennais did not feel that he was violating the basic principles of his system; only the institutional framework had changed. The people still needed to love God if they were to free themselves. They still needed the unity and sense of duty that religion could provide. Now the problem was how to persuade the people to love God when the Church was against them.

This was Lamennais' thought. He expressed it in many letters during the years 1832 and 1833. In 1833 he wrote *Paroles d'un Croyant* (*Words of a Believer*), which vividly summed up his views. But he did not publish the book. Except for a few times, he kept quiet. He had all the ideas that ultimately served to separate him from the Church, but he did not yet know what to do with them. Even his disciples were unaware of the extent to which he had drifted from orthodoxy. They knew he was troubled; they knew he maintained his political views; but they did not know that he had changed his thinking on the Church itself.

There were many reasons for Lamennais' silence. It was easier to talk of the blindness of the Church than to break with it. Traditional ties and friendships bound him still. He was tired, wanted peace, sought to avoid trouble. Furthermore, he did not wish to attack religion. While religious renovation was needed, it might come naturally, under God's guidance. The best course was to submit to the old Church in the areas of dogma and discipline, while maintaining sufficient independence to work for the reform of human society in terms of liberty for all and the improve-

ment of the conditions of the poor. Lamennais never intended a formal rebellion against the Church. For several
months he hesitated to speak out publicly even on the political issues that he had long felt did not come under Church
jurisdiction.

While Lamennais was silent his opponents were not.
Bishops continued to speak out against Mennaisian doctrines. Several writers, including former disciples, criticized
Lamennais constantly. Their comments covered not only the
doctrines of liberal Catholicism but also Lamennais' philosophical principles—and these the pope had not mentioned.
Catholic newspapers, such as the *Ami de la Religion,* kept
up a steady stream of attack. In addition to published criticisms, there was a constant barrage of rumor designed to
discredit Lamennais and his followers. These critics, not
content just to challenge Mennaisian doctrines, also sought
to question Lamennais' obedience to the Church. Time and
time again they pointed out that Lamennais had not formally adhered to *Mirari vos,* whereas many of his colleagues
had done so. Outright accusations of disobedience were
common.

It was a nasty campaign. His opponents hounded Lamennais unmercifully. Lamennais, always sensitive but always
belligerent, could not fail to see the indignity of these attacks, added to the papal condemnation. As before, the
campaign involved distortions of Lamennais' position, invention of false letters, and citations of earlier publications to
condemn more recent ones. Again, Lamennais had aroused
bitter and ugly hatred in the French Church. But, as before,
his enemies were largely correct. Lamennais was disobedi-
ent, at least privately. He had not changed his views and
was working on a book more radical than anything he had
yet done; rumors of this seeped out. He had criticized the
pope, though not yet in public. All of this is true. What
remains uncertain is this: how much did the campaign

against Lamennais force him into the open? Would he have preferred to remain silent? Did he ultimately act to strike against his opponents? Lamennais certainly felt unjustly hounded. He was driven to efforts to relieve the pressure, efforts he later felt he had to repudiate. But that he could have remained silent, even without the campaign against him, is doubtful. He had a mission for humanity and could not be deterred. He would have spoken out.

Lamennais' position in the Church began to deteriorate still further about the middle of 1833. Metternich's agents seized some of his letters and transmitted them (with some distortions) to the pope. More important, in May Montalembert translated the *Livre des Pélerins Volonais* (*The Book of Polish Pilgrims*) by the revolutionary poet Adam Mickiewicz. The translation was accompanied by a preface praising the forces of revolution and condemning all kings as oppressors of the people—public evidence that the Mennaisian group had not abandoned their views on society despite papal condemnation. Here was confirmation of the attacks by Lamennais' opponents. It was time for the Church authorities to take further action.

In May and again in October 1833 Gregory sent letters about Lamennais to French bishops. In the first he chastised Lamennais for his failure to submit fully, and in the second he gave a definite formula for submission, involving belief and advocacy of nothing contrary to the doctrines of the papacy. The earlier recourse of silence was no longer sufficient. Many old disciples established their orthodoxy by publishing statements of adherence to the papal formula; the movement had shrunk to almost nothing.

Lamennais at first wrote to the pope defending his earlier idea that a Catholic had to submit to the pope in theology and discipline but was free in politics and philosophy.* He clearly hoped to remain in the Church, although inactively,

* See Appendix A, 30.

and still be able to work for the regeneration of society. But his statement was unacceptable both to the papacy and to Lamennais' many enemies in France. The slander against Lamennais mounted. Late in 1833 the Bishop of Rennes, the head of Lamennais' diocese, forbade Lamennais to exercise the priestly functions in his area. The Breton congregation Lamennais had founded was deeply divided by this attack. The whole school system that Jean Lamennais directed was threatened by the pressures on the Mennaisian movement. So bitter was the situation that Lamennais had to leave Brittany, to protect his brother and to evade the intense local enmity. He abandoned his beloved La Chesnaie for good. His position was intolerable; he was accomplishing nothing for his doctrines, yet he was subject to the same attack as if he was working for them actively. Something had to be done.

On December 11, 1833, in Paris, Lamennais signed the papal formula. He acted on impulse. He had been in bad health, spending many sleepless nights; his mood changed often. He wanted a respite from the press campaign against him. His friends, including Gerbet and Montalembert, urged him on. They wanted to save him from his doubts, and they wanted to resolve their own conflict between loyalty to him and devotion to the Church. The Archbishop of Paris had seen Lamennais frequently and advised him to yield; Lamennais was responsive to his kind attention. And he simply could not decide to cut his final ties to the Church. So he yielded. The crisis could have been over.

Lamennais quickly regretted his move. His opponents still tormented him, either by rejoicing over his defeat or by insinuating that his submission was insincere. More important, Lamennais felt he had betrayed himself and his mission. He still believed that he had a duty to humanity, a duty that even the Church could not impede. A constant theme in his letters of early 1834 was that his reputation and his loyalty were both in doubt. He talked of the need to avoid the impression that he had connived "in the horrible system of tyranny which today burdens the people everywhere."[2] He had to purify himself in the eyes of his beloved people. And his mission came from God, not from the Church. He could not let his personal desire for peace interfere with his obligation to solace the masses and show them the way to a more perfect society.

He still believed, furthermore, that his social duty was compatible with his attachment to the Church, even with his submission to the papacy. In a way, this was self-delusion. Lamennais wrote of his resolve never to publish anything on Catholic discipline or on theology. Despite repeated evidence that the Church would not be content with this, particularly from a priest, he maintained that his interests were now purely political and that the Church had no control over this. Well after 1834 Lamennais asserted that he had never broken with the Church; there were even reports that he still went to mass as late as 1836. He was torn between his conflicting interests. He still tried to deceive himself that he had not abandoned his past, a sign of his inner conflict but also renewed proof of his independence. Lamennais sought to determine whether or not he was a loyal Catholic; he would not leave this to the Church. He knew that he was defying both the existing Church and his own friends. He hoped that he would not completely lose his old ties, but he was willing to do so for the sake of his high mission.

In April 1834 Lamennais published *Paroles d'un Croyant,** his declaration of love for mankind. A fervent book, its Old Testament style reflected Lamennais' feeling that he was a direct representative of God. It was beautifully written; Lamennais said that the printers who worked on the book could not wait to grab each page as it came off the press. It was written for the people, using a vivid style and

* See Appendix A, *31–34;* Appendix B, *5.*

soaring allegory to convey its message. The book summed up
Lamennais' social thought as it had developed over the previous five years. It was designed to console mankind in its
present misery, to offer hope for a better future, and to guide
the people toward this future.

Paroles d'un Croyant breathed hatred for the present
order. It bitterly condemned kings and other oppressors of
the poor. Their reign was doomed. The message of hope that
Christ brought to mankind was now applied to society on
earth. The divine principles of love and charity would be
the basis of the new order. Evil could not be totally abolished; man's sins would still be evident in society. But the
new society would be as close to perfection as was possible
for humanity. Men would be free from the control of other
men and, for the most part, from the hardships of poverty.
They would be united in their obedience to God and to the
divine precepts. Old jealousies and divisions would end. A
whole people, freely worshiping God and respecting one
another—this was the near utopia that Lamennais predicted.

In its denunciations of the present, in its visions of the
future, *Paroles d'un Croyant* was a revolutionary book. Yet
it did not urge revolution. In fact, it counseled respect for
property and the rights of others. Lamennais, never a revolutionary in the sense of being an advocate of disorder, had
always as his concern the establishment of durable principles for society. Now he saw three associated forces for
change, none of which had to lead to outright rebellion.
First, the people were improving themselves; Lamennais advised further development of virtue in the masses. Second,
the people were uniting. Lamennais saw clearly that oppression could continue only while the masses failed to realize
their power of numbers. Finally, God was guiding the whole
process of change. The basis for attaining the new society
was the union of God and people.

There was no mention of the Church in the book. God was

acting directly through the masses; the Church had been by-passed. Lamennais had written a passage depicting the pope, an old man, surrounded by evil monarchs, but he suppressed it in the published version. This was a non-Catholic book. Lamennais' vision of a new religion, more appropriate for the future order, was implicit in its pages.

Paroles d'un Croyant caused a real sensation. Liberal papers condemned its revolutionary tone, seeing its concern for poverty as a sign of socialism. The Catholic press was aghast. Here was confirmation of all they had been saying about Lamennais' disobedience to the pope. All of Lamennais' old opponents received new material for their denunciations. Metternich pressed the pope for action, though this time no special pressure was necessary. Gregory told the Austrian ambassador that the book was "a work of the most shameful and wild impiety, a profession of faith of a complete revolutionary."[3] Certainly Lamennais had showed almost complete unconcern for earlier papal admonitions. A new condemnation was almost inevitable.

The encyclical *Singulari nos** was issued to castigate Lamennais. It referred to Lamennais clearly now. It disapproved of his latest book. More important, it condemned the Mennaisian philosophy of general reason, as contrary to the proper authority of the Church in the determination of truth. The two pillars of Lamennais' system, his philosophy and his social thought, were now formally disavowed.

Lamennais did not take the encyclical seriously. He dismissed it as a politically inspired document and long refused public comment upon it. He claimed that he was still a loyal Catholic. For several years he still practiced Catholicism, at least occasionally.

His disciples were not so cavalier. *Singulari nos* completed the destruction of the Mennaisian movement. Almost everyone who had been associated with Lamennais at any period

---

* See Appendix C, 2.

was now forced to adhere publicly to the encyclical if they wished to preserve their orthodoxy. Most of the members of Lamennais' order submitted. Even Jean Lamennais renounced his brother. Lacordaire, of course, submitted. Gerbet, with great sorrow, did the same; eventually he, too, wrote in opposition to his former master. De Coux broke his remaining ties with Lamennais. Finally, at the end of 1834, Montalembert sent his submission to both papal encyclicals. He, like his former colleagues, realized that Lamennais had rejected the institutional Church, despite his professions of attachment. They could not join him; they had never intended to abandon the Church, but rather to enhance its power. The decision was not easy. The personal loyalty to Lamennais was great; the desire for liberty and some new social order was intense. However, neither could rival the importance of devotion to the Catholic religion.

Lamennais himself kept working until his death in 1854. He wrote a number of political tracts, along the lines of *Paroles d'un Croyant*, and he continued to develop his general philosophy. He served in the revolutionary assembly in 1848. Neither his activity nor his importance ended with his break with the Church. After 1834, however, he was merely one of many intellectual agitators in France, and by no means the most important. His preaching of religion without a Church made little sense; and again, it was only one of many such systems being advocated in France at the time. Lamennais' real contributions, his historical importance, came within the framework of Catholicism. The crisis of his life was the prolonged confrontation of his doctrines with the official Church. His renunciation of the Church, complete by 1836, set him on a new course.

Lamennais' crisis had been intensely personal. It involved agonizing conflicts of loyalty and entailed a deliberate renunciation of the past. Lamennais' pathetic efforts to claim that he was still a Catholic showed the price that this renunciation demanded. It was not easy to break almost all the old ties, at the age of fifty-two. Yet the crisis was not Lamennais' alone. Thousands of his followers faced similar dilemmas. The whole Church was affected. Lamennais had forced doctrinal decisions that guided the Church for many decades to come. In France particularly he had provoked a new and decisive split between the Church and the revolutionary heritage. The crisis of the early 1830's was a failure for all parties. Lamennais did not succeed in converting the Church, so he had to abandon it. His followers chose another course, but they, too, failed to reconcile the Church and modern society. On the surface, Lamennais' enemies had won. They had driven Lamennais and his doctrines from the Church. Yet their opposition had blinded them to the reality of the problems Lamennais raised. They succeeded in banning change within the Church. They failed to see that Lamennais was right on one point at least: change was inevitable.

CHAPTER VII

———————

CONCLUSION

Lamennais' Catholic career was devoted to the reconciliation of the Church and modern society, to the benefit of both. Initially he sought a novel formula for Catholic truth, capable of winning modern skeptics. To this extent concessions had to be made to the spirit of the age; pure tradition would not do. But Lamennais directed his early efforts primarily at convincing non-Catholics of the error of their ways. Gradually he came to see more merit in modern trends. By 1830 he had shifted the desired reconciliation more to the terms of modern society, less to those of the Church. "Modern society"—liberal thought, as Lamennais interpreted it—was opposed to the union of Church and state; so this union had to be abandoned, despite its support both by tradition and by the majority of the members of the French Church. "Modern society" wanted liberty of thought; therefore the Church had to accept and even urge liberty of the press and education. These liberties would benefit the Church itself. But what Lamennais ignored, again, was the opposition of most Catholics to innovations involving liberty for error. Lamennais consistently urged an adaptation both immediate and radical.

Lamennais' liberal Catholicism was doomed from the start. It relied on a pure liberalism that most French liberals

143

would not accept. It relied on a willingness of the Church to innovate on all fronts. Most Catholics recognized that the Church was in a period of crisis. But instead of trying new means to meet the crisis, they wished to cling ever more tightly to old. In a confused era it was best to trust in what had worked in the past. Lamennais was reduced to claiming Catholicity for a movement opposed by the institutional Church at all levels. He tried to claim papal support, against the French hierarchy and the older clergy. When papal support failed, he talked of direct contact with God, with the people, with a true Church that was different from the existing body. Finally, he stopped working within the Church altogether.

What had Lamennais accomplished? Any biography must try to establish the historical importance of its central figure. What if Lamennais had not existed? Would society or the Church, or even just the French Church, have been any different? The question is a difficult one. Most of the figures prominent in history have been successful, at least to some degree. Lamennais had a compelling personality and intellect; but he failed. He has been compared to Marx as a prophet and thinker in his period. It is true that both men saw something of the basic direction of the society of their day. But Marx founded his own, independent movement. Lamennais, trying to impel a large and highly traditional institution, was unable to do so, and he left little behind him. His disciples abandoned him. He organized nothing to succeed him. Only his writings remain, and though they have been elaborately studied, they are not widely read.

Within the Catholic Church, Lamennais left little mark. The intense hatred he stirred up did not extend beyond his own generation. Many of his doctrines were forgotten. His philosophy, on which he placed so much hope for the intellectual regeneration of the Church, had only limited and transitory success. The papal condemnation killed it almost entirely.

Lamennais' liberal Catholicism did have greater influence. In Belgium, where the Church was clearly persecuted until 1830, his doctrines had great appeal. Lamennais did not initiate liberal Catholicism in Belgium, but he gave it firm intellectual support during its early period. In France his influence was felt less directly. Liberal Catholicism did not die with the end of the Mennaisian movement; it continued, but with less bombast and inflexibility. It still owed something to Lamennais, if only an awareness of the central problems in the relationship between the Church and modern society. And some of the leaders of later liberalism in the Church had been, at least briefly, under Lamennais' influence. Such men as Lacordaire and Montalembert had been liberals before they encountered Lamennais. Although they firmly renounced Lamennais, they had learned from him. But liberal Catholicism was a minority movement in France even later in the century, and Lamennais was not its primary source.

The ultramontanism that Lamennais advocated for a decade and a half had a brilliant future. Lamennais was not the only early ultramontane, but he was among the most vigorous; and he did help convert a whole generation of younger clergy to its doctrines. Here he was clearly working with the times. The revolution, while attaching the Church to the state in new ways, released forces that could only loosen the ties. The state could not be firmly devoted to the interests of the Church. The Restoration clergy largely ignored this fact, because of traditional loyalties and the apparent sympathy of the government. But under the July Monarchy the diffidence of the state was unmistakable. There was no need for a Church-state break. However, the French clergy did need some independent unity; this could best come from Rome. And the papacy was consistently interested in strengthening the Church in a hostile age by centralization of power. Ultramontanism gained in France, but it became attached to clerical conservatism, to a desire to resist change. It did not serve the sort of Catholic regeneration Lamennais had intended.

The basic point is, then, that Lamennais was working against the fundamental trends within the Church. He came to see this, but was powerless to reverse the tide. The conservatism of the Church in the early nineteenth century was almost inevitable. In France the age of the Catholic leaders, their social station, and their direct memory of the attacks of the revolution dictated a firm resistance to further change. Even under the July Monarchy, it seemed best to rely on a government that at least promised to protect religion against major popular hostility. For the Church generally, conservatism was still more logical. There were the Papal States to defend; the threat to them came from a revolutionary liberalism. More important, since outside of France most regimes remained largely traditional, there was no clear reason to anticipate a revolutionary victory. Concessions to liberalism would weaken sympathetic governments, without bringing any assurance of greater liberal favor to the Church.

Because a defensive mentality dominated, aside from a few special cases, such as Belgium, the bulk of Lamennais' program was vigorously rejected. It made no sense to most churchmen. It is possible that, without Lamennais' forcing an explicit statement, the papacy would have maintained some ambiguity toward liberal ideas, without approving them. Gregory had been willing to tolerate such ambiguity. But Lamennais was not forcing a determination of policy, merely a statement of it.

Even in France the liberal Catholic movement did not die. It was eclipsed, but emerged again in the 1840's. The Church again rejected it. The condemnation of Lamennais confirmed the opinion of most liberals that the Church was their implacable foe, but they had thought so all along. Lamennais did not influence the Church in the way he intended. He roused great opposition, but even this did not alter the main lines of Catholic policy. The opposition merely revealed the policy.

Lamennais was a prophet. His vision of modern society was in many ways correct. Most of his French biographers, including many Catholics in the twentieth century, have hailed the farsightedness of his view. He was correct in saying that, in France at least, the Church should be separate from the state. When the state forced this separation, in 1905, it proved to be mutually beneficial, by largely removing the Church from political contentions. He was right in saying that the Church should accommodate itself to liberty. Again, in France and elsewhere, it has largely done so and with good results. He was right in urging the Church to come to grips with modern science and philosophy. His own system has been forgotten, but he pointed to real problems with which the Church has dealt actively since the 1880's. Lamennais said that the people were drifting from Catholicism because the Church no longer spoke to their real problems. He was right, although he exaggerated the alienation from the Church in his own day. But the masses did become interested in improving their economic lot; they did come to feel that the Church was unsympathetic to their demands. Particularly in the cities, many left the Church entirely and many more lost any fervor for religion. By the end of the century the Church began to recognize this problem and, haltingly, began to develop a social program. Was Lamennais right in his assertion that society, for its part, needed religion to survive? This is one point that is not yet susceptible to a historical answer. What is clear is that Lamennais was correct in predicting where society was heading in its relation with the Church. By 1900, even more in the present day, many leaders of the Church had come to share his sense of the principal problems of Catholicism.

Lamennais' prophetic sense is one of the main attractions of his biography. He loved to foretell. His solutions were not always correct, certainly they were usually unrealistic; but still he had his vision of the movement of modern society. To go from this to a claim that he influenced Catholicism in later decades would be unrealistic. Some modern Catholics may cite Lamennais because they see the same issues he saw. But for the most part, their views are independently derived. When the Church began to adjust as Lamennais had urged, by the end of the nineteenth century, its leaders did not reread Lamennais. The problems were by then so obvious that little historical sense was required. It can be argued that the Church would have been better off had it listened to Lamennais earlier, but the fact is that it did not and there were good reasons for its attitudes. And Lamennais did lack some of the elements of a truly Catholic view at any time. He ignored discipline. He relied on the primacy of his own judgment. He proved to be interested in society independent of the Church, if necessary at the expense of the Church. His claim to prophecy cannot be faulted. An attribution of important influence after his own time is wrong.

What is left, then? First, through Lamennais a good picture emerges of the state of religion and society in his age, precisely because the man was a prophet. He was wrong about what the Church could do, but the opposition he raised shows what the Church would do in its contact with modern trends. He pinpointed the crucial problems of Catholicism in an era of revolutionary social and political change.

He did, in a minor way, hamper the adjustment he sought. He was unable to appeal to non-Catholics in any significant number; they considered him amusing. Yet he was too inflexible to attract most active Catholics in his day. He was incapable of urging subtle change. He could not cater to fixed prejudices while working around them for a recognition of social change. He lacked a sense of tactics, in an institution in which tactics are all-important. His radicalism justified many of the objections to liberal Catholicism. It could and did appeal to many who saw the same crisis that he saw; it could not attract an organization that still had established positions to defend.

Finally, Lamennais is interesting for himself. He was not simply a prophet ignored or a device through which a broader situation can be understood. He was a brilliant and troubled man. He was raised outside the training of his priestly profession. This helped him to understand some of the trends beyond the Church, but did not allow him fully to understand the demands of his own calling. His was a tortured personality. He needed guidance and sympathy, but did not always find them. He lived within himself, in a starkly intellectual atmosphere. For a long time Catholicism offered him a framework in which he could find the solace and intellectual challenge he required. He never merged with the Church. He built his systems on his own; his intuitions of the future were his own. His brilliance and sensitivity carried him to prominence in Catholicism. His own experience in the Church alternately exalted and depressed him. Finally, he developed his own vision. His love for God and the Church was transformed to love for God and the people. His intellectual independence was preserved, though his practical influence waned.

Lamennais might have succeeded had he been willing to limit himself. He might have taught the French Church that liberty in teaching and association could only be beneficial. He would have needed a patience he did not possess. He would have had to have abandoned more general demands for Church-state separation. For this achievement Lamennais would have been satisfied only if he had worked for the Church alone. He did not. Lamennais wanted the Church to gain, but not for its own sake. The Church had to lead society for democratic and social reform; it had to go beyond a conventional religious function. His was a total view of society; compromise for the sake of one institution was needless. He went beyond Catholicism, beyond liberal Catholicism, though he worked for both. He was isolated, but only because he sought to reconcile values that in the nineteenth century proved incompatible.

The creative part of his life was devoted to fighting the trends, though he did not know it. The movements with which he tried to deal were hostile to the Church; the Church was hostile to them. Lamennais could not break this mutual enmity. Can an individual ever do so?

POSTSCRIPT

Lamennais' later years were unhappy ones in many ways. His doctrines, his life's mission, did not gain ground. Although he had many supporters, he was not a leader in movements of opposition to the established order. And over the established order he had no influence at all. His vision of the future remained bright, but he was bitterly disappointed over the course of French politics. In addition, his health continued to trouble him, though he lived to the age of seventy-two. Now suffering from persistent financial difficulties, he lived very simply, even meagerly.

Lamennais' views changed little after 1834; he had finally found the approach that suited him. He continued to defend the poor against the selfishness of the rich and the oppression of the state, urging material justice and political democracy. But, unlike most republicans and socialists, he wanted more than this; he still sought a new religion as the basis for the more perfect society. This religion, having its roots in traditional Christianity, would be essentially new.

Lamennais' problem at this point was not doctrinal but practical. He had found the truth, but how was he to spread it? He wrote a variety of pamphlets and some longer treatises expounding his views and worked on the fringes of some republican groups. He was jailed for a year in 1841 for a particularly vigorous attack on the foreign and internal policies of the July Monarchy. He published four more volumes of general philosophy and translated the gospels with a commentary showing how they suggested the new religion; later he translated the whole New Testament as well as Dante's *Divine Comedy*. He established a newspaper, but it was unsuccessful.

None of this work had much impact, though Lamennais still had a considerable reputation. He professed to enjoy his new life. He did make some new friends, and above all he was sustained by his certainty that he had chosen the right course. He never resumed contact with his past. In 1836 he wrote a book on his relations with the papacy to bring to a close this phase of his life. He rebuffed overtures by a few old friends and by his brother, Jean. When Pius IX became pope in 1846, and seemed inclined toward liberalism, several liberal churchmen in Rome urged Lamennais to return to the Church. Lamennais replied that he wished the pope well but had no interest in changing his own views. He doubted that the pope could undertake real reform, as, indeed, Pius IX did not.

The Revolution of 1848 gave Lamennais a final opportunity to play a significant role. He started a newspaper, *Le Peuple Constituant,* which lasted for five months. He was elected to the Assembly in April, from the Paris region, and then was chosen to serve on the constitutional committee; his reputation was still a mighty one. Lamennais urged a constitution that would provide universal suffrage and universal, gratuitous education, destruction of the University monopoly, separation of Church and state, local liberties as opposed to domination by the central government, and a system of graduated taxes. No one listened to him—he was always a poor speaker anyway—and he soon resigned from the committee. The revolution did not fulfill Lamennais' expectations. The poor people were defeated; Lamennais never urged them to violence, but he was bitterly opposed to the repression practiced during the June Days. The Church, gaining new political powers, became increasingly conservative. An authoritarian government under Louis Napoleon took control of France. Lamennais condemned all this, but he was powerless to do anything about it.

Lamennais died in 1854. His death provided a final small bit of drama. He refused to see old Church friends, and when, on his deathbed, they urged him to see a priest, Lamennais refused: "No, no, no—leave me in Peace."[1] At his own request he was buried in a common, unmarked grave. A large number of poor people and a big police guard attended his funeral. There was a slight scuffle around the grave. No one made any speeches. A gravedigger asked if there should be a cross placed on the grave, and was told no. Someone shouted: "Everyone can go home, it's all over."[2]

APPENDIX A

EXCERPTS FROM LAMENNAIS' LETTERS

(Translated from *Correspondance*. 2 vols. Ed. Emile Forgues
Paris, 1864)

1. To Mlle. De Tremereuc, May 28, 1822

What grace do we not owe divine Providence! It does all things
well, as the Bible says. We almost never know what we should want or
often even what we do want; let us at least have confidence in our
heavenly Father, to believe that what He wishes is always wisest and
best. Let us adore His decrees in silence, let us adore them with love,
and let us silence all our thoughts when they differ from His.

2. To Marquis de Coriolis, April 30, 1825

Everything is being prepared for a change of scene and, for myself,
I think we are reaching the catastrophe of this terrible drama. . . .
There is uneasiness everywhere, disgust, scorn, indignation. Discontent
is growing daily, people's minds are becoming bitter and hot; there is a
storm in the future. It would be fortunate to find a little solitude under
a mild climate, far from Europe, in a peaceful region if there are any,
where one could live in a Christian way, sheltered from the revolutions
that menace the world.

3. To same, October 12, 1825

And this year 1825 is not yet over. Men's minds are becoming
precipitous and precipitate society into an abyss whose depth is unknown. I defy all the parties to say what they want; only imbeciles
would try to answer. Men work blindly to destroy, and that's all.
Success in this venture has been so great that there are not any

elements left to rebuild after the inevitable upheaval that threatens us in the near future. Now, all efforts are united against Religion; it is the only enemy that is feared. . . . On all sides there is pressure for a break with Rome and the establishment of a national Church, of a representative Church, which would represent only folly, dangerous opinions, practical doubts, the meanness and cowardice of the present day. They are persecuting order even in the bosom of God. Certainly the world has never seen anything like this, and we will see more yet; this is only the beginning.

4. To Comte de Senfft-Pilsach, March 18, 1826

The future is entirely in the moral state of the people, a state that is itself only the natural and progressive development of doctrines that derive from a remote past. The Government, to save itself, would have to change its own essence, an impossible thing and one that in any case it will never understand. What is radically vicious never reforms itself; and I am not speaking of the forms of the *Government,* the only question that concerns opinion today, perhaps because there is nothing more banal. Society is dying; people are arguing and fighting to know how to clothe the corpse, for it is certainly clear that the disease is in his costume; wise men don't stop saying this from one end of Europe to the other. My friend, why fool ourselves? We are at the beginning of an immense revolution, which will end either with the death or with the rebirth of the people, but which will last, whatever happens, as long as there remains some perceptible remnant of the great cadaver whose dissolution began in 1789.

5. To same, December 22, 1826

I am ashamed to say it—but I don't think I'm being conceited—by the pure effect of circumstances I find myself the center of those who love and defend Religion in this country. If I were gone, everything would dissolve. I am working to make something survive me, and I hope to succeed, despite innumerable obstacles. If I abandoned the work, it would collapse immediately. Would I not be responsible then before God? There are many good elements, but scattered and weak; it is like a seed that must be carefully cultivated to develop. . . . [On our religious situation], the government is disposed to do all that the revolutionaries ask, provided that they do not push it too quickly. They have forbidden all civil and military employees in Lyons to attend the erection of the cross, so that this has not taken place. The prefects are instructed to watch the clergy closely and to send notes on all the priests. This is a preparatory measure. They haven't yet decided to act against the missions, in spite of definite resolutions about this in the cabinet. The fate of the Jesuits is set; only the execution of the dissolution causes problems. . . . They will succumb without any doubt, and they will succumb without honor. . . . Almost universal opinions hold that the order is finished; it has nothing in it that corresponds to the situation and the present needs of society.

As to the secular clergy, the majority is excellent. It is difficult to imagine the extent to which all the Catholic doctrines have penetrated this group in just the last year. The more I think about it, the more I see a real marvel here. The number of devoted priests seems double what it was formerly, and truth makes progress every day. But here is the other side of the coin. The Ministry of Religion works ardently to corrupt all the sources of teaching. It threatens and dismisses some, seduces others, and this system in the long run will bring bad results, especially when the episcopate, already so weak, is constituted according to the views of the government. Two bishops have just been named: one, M. Savy, was headmaster of the college of Toulouse, a detestable establishment; the other, M. de Villeneuve, lived more like a layman than like a priest, walking around Paris in trousers, etc. All the posts are given to men of this type.

Another very great evil is Saint-Sulpice, where young men of all dioceses are trained. Gallicanism dominates there and from there supports all its partisans in the provinces.

6. To Comtesse de Senfft-Pilsach, May 2, 1827

It's been three weeks since I've read any papers, so that I am entirely ignorant of what is happening; but I'm told that everything is going along as usual, that is, from bad to worse. I have long been persuaded that a general revolution is inevitable, and that all the efforts of good men should be directed to the future. The bases of a new society must be posed in advance; the old one is rotten, it is dead; it will not be revived. It is folly to count on the governments, which are no longer governments and cannot become so again. We must work with the people, which is always possible, until the time set by God for the consummation of things. The Church has a great mission and it will fulfill it; but the moment has not yet come; however, it cannot be far off.

7. To Comte de Senfft-Pilsach, November 19, 1827

Nothing is done today, and nothing is supported, by institutions. Events are determined by certain ideas, certain passions that ferment in the masses and overwhelm everything. . . . Is this not the real cause of the fact that certain governments, really almost all of them, try in vain to destroy a liberty [the liberty of the press] that is stronger than they are because it is truly a *necessity* of present society? Governments are everywhere revolutionary or anticlerical by their doctrines and often by their systems and habits of administration. But what is censorship in such hands? There are truths that must be established and errors that must be exhausted. Freedom of the press is essential for this double purpose. It will doubtless do much harm, but this passing harm is itself part of the designs of Providence, which can build only on ground free of ruins. [It is a great error] to accept the evil that exists and defend it for fear that, if it is touched, a worse evil will follow.

8. *To Comtesse de Senfft-Pilsach, November 14, 1828*

I have said what I feel to be true, what I cannot feel is not true, and this satisfies my conscience. I am fighting almost everyone: liberals, royalists, princes, ministers, and I am sure that the near future will justify what I am telling them. There is no reason to be tactful in these times of universal dissolution. All of Society is exhausted. Why flatter this invalid? I tell him that he will die, but I show him further on a possible resurrection, which the now inevitable disorders, calamities, will serve to hasten, according to the laws of Providence. . . . The further I go, the more I am persuaded that no good can be effected henceforward without great catastrophes. An immense liberty is indispensable for the truths that will save the world, to develop as they should; and sovereigns correctly judge that this liberty would kill them instantly. They therefore struggle against it with all their strength, but Society's need for it is too great for them to struggle long with success. What will happen? The irresistible force that has carried them along will break them.

9. *To Comte de Senfft-Pilsach, January 11, 1829*

I am fully convinced that Society cannot be cured by ordinary means; that the governments, altered in their principle, can neither regenerate it nor regenerate themselves; that therefore an entire, absolute dissolution is inevitable and that thus one should consider it less in itself than in its consequences, seeing in it one of these admittedly terrible crises that are necessary to the renewal of life, according to the eternal laws of the moral world. When a certain number of men, firmly grasping certain truths that are the basis of order, will unite among themselves, then the seed of a new society will exist and that strength that will necessarily prevail in their midst will prevail, and promptly, over all the disordered or antisocial forces. To reach this point, two things are necessary: to enlighten minds by discussion and to strengthen spirits by combat. Hence liberty, possessed or sought, is today the first need of the people and the indispensable condition of salvation. If the Government placed itself at the head of such a movement it would save us and save itself. But can it? I do not know. What I do know is that it won't want to. Therefore everything must be done by the people, that is, by a new people, gradually formed under the influence of a better conceived Christianity, amid the nations in ruins.

10. *To Mme. Yemeniz, March 24, 1829*

In matters of a religious nature: have I departed from the teaching of Rome? Then I condemn myself. Haven't I merely exposed and developed the constant doctrines of the Roman Pontiffs? Then no real Catholic can condemn me, for he would condemn, under my name, the Holy See itself.

11. *To Comte de Senfft-Pilsach, July 13, 1830*

The clergy, or at least part of it, and nearly all the bishops, look and do not see, listen and do not hear, plunged as they are in their old and stupid prejudices. Binding the cause of religion inseparably to that of the Government which oppresses it, they are preparing a general apostasy with all their might; they can only expect a violent persecution, if irritated liberalism triumphs, or shameful and heavy chains if the opposite party wins: this is their profound and noble politics. Besides, everything indicates a dissolution, and the punishment will soon follow the crime. Then some enlightenment will gradually come, for man is so made that sunlight leaves him in the dark; he discerns nothing save by the glow of fires that consume and devastate.

12. *To Comtesse de Senfft-Pilsach, August 6, 1830*

You will have learned from the newspapers about the events of these last fifteen days. They have been foreseen for too long to surprise anyone.

Charles X and his supporters wanted to lose; they have lost. The question is now decided forever. Some people who were devoted to them are astonished and stupified, but there is very little real regret. If they are wise, they will enter frankly into the new destinies, for the past is irrevocable. The Duke of Orleans is going to receive the crown; it will be heavy on his head. Most people would prefer a Republic frankly declared, and I am one of them. But I hope that the royalty will be purely nominal. If one lets the man who bears the title of King have even a hope of real power, immediately war will begin between him and the republican party. . . . Anyway, we are very calm in Brittany, up to now. We must wait and see. We can't predict anything yet.

13. *To Baron de Vitrolles, August 27, 1830*

The Revolution, in its political aspect, is a universal reaction of the people against arbitrary government, that is, the government that is conventionally called absolute. Its definitive result will be to overturn this government everywhere, to put free institutions in its place, under some form or other, and this result will be good in itself. But to obtain it in reality and to achieve a stable state, we need a principle of order and stability that is totally lacking today. This principle is Religion. We should thus tend to unite Religion and Liberty; moreover, there is no way to preserve Religion itself other than to free it from dependence on the temporal power, so that in this respect too we should want and demand Liberty, which is salvation itself. So much for the future.

For the present, two things are evident: first, that the immense majority of the nation rejects despotism or absolute government; second, that it fears anarchy. But the only way to avoid it, if it is possible, or at least to abridge it, is to organize an active resistance against it by uniting and organizing those who fear it, a union that can be effected only in the sense of the general opinion, that is, by the application of the principle of liberty. . . . For myself, I believe that every honest man, forgetting what cannot be saved, should support the government which still maintains and can alone today maintain a remnant of order. . . . You realize that personally, silence and inaction would be most suitable to my tastes in all respects; that I do not hope to be understood immediately and that thus, in speaking, I am obeying only what seems to me to be an imperious duty.

14. *To Comtesse de Senfft-Pilsach, November 16, 1830*

The new Government will not or cannot depart from the position that destroyed its predecessor; thus it is without force. Everyone says "this cannot last" and everyone is right. But what will we have afterward? To this, there is no answer. The future is as black as a night in January. For myself, I do not believe in the possibility of any stable government for a long time. And I think that this interval should be used to conquer the true and great liberties that will be the necessary foundation of the future order that is coming.

15. To same, December 5, 1830

Our newspaper is producing a great effect, one that far surpasses what we expected. I hope that it will contribute powerfully to the reconciliation of all Frenchmen and that it will effect the complete liberation of the Catholics. Associations are being formed everywhere to demand the promised liberties by all legal means, which are our right as they are the right of everyone. Doubtless we will encounter opposition, but this opposition is our strength, for strength develops only by combat. . . . Public opinion is for us, and it is fine to defend, in the presence of France, the cause of all Frenchmen. For what we wish, what we demand, what we will obtain sooner or later, is equal liberty for all.

16. To Comte de Senfft-Pilsach, December 23, 1830

What shall we say of the Church? Let it rise great once again, when God sends the man who is to found the last epoch of human society here below. I see this man and I will not see him; I am present at the creation of what his word will effect, and my eyes will not witness it. But how beautiful it is, even at the distance from which we view it. How fine it is to think that perhaps we can cooperate in some way to prepare this marvelous spectacle.

17. To Contessa Fernanda Riccini, January 14, 1831

I cannot leave France. Not that I plan to rest here; on the contrary, because a priest is called to sustain a great fight and fulfill a magnificent mission. It is time that we recognize the hand of God in the events that are changing the face of the world today, that despite the disorders inevitable to periods of transition one can penetrate in some manner to the long-hidden principle of this extraordinary movement, which is nothing but the reaction of Catholicism against brute force, and a manifest intervention of Providence to save the world by freeing the Church. This will become more evident daily and the prejudices that prevent us from seeing it are one of the causes that most retard the triumph of order or of Chrisianity. But, I repeat, the day will dawn, and we should await with patience the timing of God.

18. To Cardinal Weld, February 27, 1831

In the grave situation of Europe and of France in particular, it is the duty of Catholics called to defend Religion, and a stricter duty still for priests, to make sure that they do not depart from the Faith, and consequently to have recourse to the supreme Pastor to receive humbly from his mouth the infallible oracles of the eternal Truth. This is what the editors of the *Avenir* are doing today; they hope that you will place the declaration of their doctrines at the feet of the Holy Father, urging him to correct them if they have involuntarily fallen into some error, in which case they would hasten to give their retraction all possible publicity. For they hold nothing so dear as to show themselves most docile and most devoted children of the common Father.

19. To Mgr. de Pins, Archbishop of Amasie, August 15, 1831

Once the questions of doctrine are separated from purely political questions, I will not deny that in treating the latter we may have said some things that have displeased Rome—not the Pontiff, but the Sovereign, bound as he is in many respects to the political system of Europe, a system from which the Church has suffered so much. I have felt this disadvantage and have deplored it; but it was inevitable, unless we subordinated eternal things to things of time and abandoned the defense of Religion among us, the defense of that which, without any doubt, the Vicar of Jesus Christ places above all else. Time, which changes positions, will also change the point of view in which he has been able to consider the direction of our thought in the order of purely human things, and will justify us in his eyes, I am confident.

20. To Comtesse de Senfft-Pilsach, November 8, 1831

Unhappily, the higher clergy is precipitating Religion into the stupid and infamous intrigues [of the royalists]; we wish to separate it from them, and a great part of the clergy supported us admirably. The bishops killed everything; they are forbidding people to read our journal; they are persecuting priests suspected of attachment to our doctrines; they are moving heaven and earth to revive Gallicanism, thus attracting a hatred against the Church whose consequences frighten me, while we have succeeded in returning even some atheists not only to the faith but also to the practice of religion. And by what means do they attack? By intrigues, interdicts, silent plots, by a terrible system of calumnies; and this opposition has found some support in Rome! Rome has leagued with its most dangerous enemies against its own doctrines and against its defenders. Without explaining, without saying a word, without giving a judgment, which we requested six months ago, very humbly, Rome has encouraged, even excited, our adversaries, who are its own. This position is not tenable. We are going to abandon the *Avenir* and the Agency. The only barrier that existed between the Government and the Church is going to fall, just at the time when the projects of the government are becoming clearer each day. . . . Victory would have been certain, and never would the Church have been stronger or freer. But no: its leaders have said it must die, it must. . . . I will stop. One cannot easily talk of the death of Religion and Society. But the seeds of life that we have planted in a number of minds will not perish; they will develop on the day marked by Providence, and this will be the day of salvation.

21. *To Marquis de Coriolis, February 7, 1832*

I think that our stay in Rome may be prolonged six weeks or two months still. Here's the situation: it is completely false that we have been disapproved by the Pope, who is most annoyed about such rumors. He hasn't pronounced one way or the other. As to the other people in Rome with whom we have had contact, not a one has raised the slightest objection either to our doctrines, which everyone here regards as perfectly Catholic, or to the manner in which we have defended Religion. The difficulties that may arise are outside these two areas, and relate only to the difficulties of the present political situation or to the fears and the hopes that everyone conceives, according to his personal prejudices, concerning future events. But, I repeat, no problems on the principles.

22. *To Comtesse de Senfft-Pilsach, February 10, 1832*

I need air, movement, faith, love, everything that one seeks in vain amid these old ruins, on which the vilest human passions crawl like immense reptiles, in shadow and silence. The Pope is pious and well intentioned, but, foreign to the world, he is completely ignorant of the state of the Church and of Society. Immobile in the shadows that people spread about him, he weeps and he prays. His role, his mission, is to prepare and hasten the last final destruction that is to precede social regeneration, and without which it would be impossible or incomplete. This is why God has put him in the hands of men lower than low, ambitious, avaricious, corrupted. . . . Be sure that we are touching on the greatest events the world has seen for a century. A frightful struggle is going to begin in all parts of Europe and the result is not in doubt, whatever the alternatives of success may be. Twenty more years of this situation and Catholicism will be dead; God will save it by the people; what do I care about the rest? My politics is the triumph of Christ; my legitimacy is His law; my country is the human race, whom He has redeemed with His blood.

23. To Marquis de Coriolis, September 15, 1832

The Princes and the Pope believe that by uniting they would stop the movement of the people and maintain them under the yoke. Gregory XVI had just proclaimed this great alliance and thereby condemned Catholics to inaction. They cannot defend the Church against the will of its leader; so we will be silent; but events will speak only too loudly, and the world will see a fine mess. But our efforts have not been lost; these are seeds that Providence has planted in Society, to develop at a better time, when others have accomplished the destruction that must come first.

24. To Charles de Coux, October 20, 1832

In the sincerity of a wholly Catholic zeal, we have tried to defend the Church in one of the greatest perils it has experienced since its beginning. The Sovereign Pontiff has disapproved of our action; we have stopped; this was our duty. And though I rejoice at the satisfaction that the Holy Father has experienced over this act of obedience, I am far from feeling meritorious; we acted as Catholics, that's all. But, now that the danger seems to be becoming more alarming by the day and by the hour; now that hatred of Catholicism and hatred of Rome increase steadily, with unparalleled rapidity; now that spirits are everywhere filled with the direst forebodings, what can I say to the Holy Father, in what words could I portray the depths of my grief? His grief is still greater, I am sure, and my silence should respect it. At the approach of the coming evils, of the tempest that will shake Christianity to its foundations, I want only one thing, to be forgotten in my obscure retreat; I cherish only one consolation, that of praying at the foot of the cross.

25. To Father Ventura, November 30, 1832

The group that is growing daily includes those who, persuaded that Religion, Faith, is one of the elements of human nature—at the same time regard Christianity as a transitory system once useful but now only an obstacle to the happiness of people and the progress of Society. [This group] awaits a new religion that, founded on broader bases and in harmony with the development of humanity, will restore men to their original unity, which Christianity has not effected, for it has exercised strong and durable influence only over Western nations; an influence, besides, mixed with good and evil, with a growing proportion of the latter.

26. To Comtesse de Senfft-Pilsach, December 15, 1832

Do not be afraid; we will see Christ again, the saving Christ, the liberating Christ, the Christ who pities the poor, the weak, the miserable, and who breaks the sword over their oppressors. Besides, from another point of view, what is the history of men if not the history of the continual development of humanity. . . .

27. To same, January 25, 1833

The world under its old form was tired out. Men had abused everything; they had denatured, corrupted everything. That is why the old Hierarchies, political and ecclesiastic, are perishing together; they are now only two specters embracing in a tomb. God, by means that are unknown to me, will doubtless regenerate His Church. It will not perish; it is immortal, for it is really the Society of the human race under the law of Redemption effected by Jesus Christ. But what will its form be when the purifying fire has consumed the dessicated envelope that now veils it from almost all eyes? I do not know.

28. To Marquis de Coriolis, July 29, 1833

My poor exhausted body will no longer endure any disturbance in its habits; it resembles the European monarchies. The kings don't care to realize it, but I don't see that they are any healthier. Yes, the clouds are getting thicker; an immense and violent storm is forming on the horizon; at the first trembling of the political atmosphere, thunder will boom from one end to the other. We are approaching the time when the last battles will take place between the people and the sovereigns.

29. To Comtesse de Senfft-Pilsach, August 1, 1833

What is best in France is the people; they have almost everywhere preserved the faith and, with exquisite good sense, have stayed outside all the political systems; but they will not long endure oppression. . . . My doctrines remain intact. It is increasingly obvious that the Pope fears and disavows my political views completely. In their relationship with the government of the Church, he is judge and I am not; he can command, I will obey. It is my duty and, thank God, I hope never to fail it. But outside the Church, in the purely temporal sphere, and most particularly in what concerns the interests of my country, I recognize no authority that has the right to impose an opinion or dictate my conduct. I say loudly that in this sphere, which is not that of the spiritual power, I will never abdicate my independence; in thought and in action, I will take advice only from my conscience and my reason.

30. To Pope Gregory XVI, August 4, 1833

I declare: First, that for all sorts of reasons but especially because it is up to the leader of the Church to judge what can be good and useful to it, I have resolved to remain, in the future, in my writings and in my actions, totally foreign to its concerns. Second, that no one, thank God, is more submitted than I, from the bottom of my heart and without any reserve, to all the decisions that have emanated or will emanate from the Apostolic Holy See, on doctrines of faith and morals and on the laws of discipline under its sovereign authority.

31. To Marquis de Coriolis, December 6, 1833

It is true, my dear friend, that clerical hatreds, roused still by political passions, are implacable. Those who persecute me know perfectly well that I am orthodox and even more than this in the religious aspect; but they need a veil to hide from the simple the real motives of the persecution with which they wish to crush me. There is also, beneath all this, a secret but powerful influence of diplomacy that is trying to reduce me to silence and to inaction. But it may soon be that circumstances will arise in which my conscience commands me to act and speak, for I have duties to my country and I will not desert them.

32. To Ange Blaize, April 27, 1834

The writing in question [Paroles d'un Croyant] is not a sudden and passing mood, but the fruit of mature reflections. It has been finished for almost a year. Neither M. Gerbet nor any of those to whom I have read it found anything in it that hurts Religion in any way; no difficulty on that point. It also does not contradict what I wrote to the Pope and told the Archbishop. I have always declared that I reserved my full liberty for anything that I felt concerned my country and humanity, and that my conscience did not permit me to collaborate even by my silence in the political system of Rome. . . . My reasons for publishing the essay are: (1) the sense that in doing so I am fulfilling a duty, because I see salvation for the world only in the union of order, right, justice, and liberty; (2) the necessity to establish my position, which, in the eyes of the public, is now equivocal and false; to cleanse my name for the future from the reproach of having connived at the horrible system of tyranny that everywhere today is weighing on the people.

33. *To Comtesse de Senfft-Pilsach, April 27, 1834*

We forget too easily that our existence below is only a battle, a grievous effort to return to the state from which we have fallen. And what is true for all of us is true for whole peoples, for all of humanity. Jesus Christ was the real representative as well as the leader of this. Who fought and suffered more than He? And all this ended, on earth, only in a tomb. A little book is going to appear that will displease you greatly . . . some should not read it, others cannot; it is not a book of the present. It is a book of instinct, of presentiment, and of conscience. The author has seen the tears streaming from the eyes of the people; he has heard their cries of suffering, and he has felt in himself a great desire to console them. He is, right or wrong, convinced that justice is lost in the world, and that no one knows what being a man means, what man's destinies are, and that man is being treated as God does not wish His creature to be treated. He believes that a new order is coming, and nothing of the past will survive, and that the only salvation from now on is in the intimate union of Justice and Liberty.

34. *To same, July 5, 1834*

I am calling for Liberty with all my power, which can be established only on the double basis of Justice and Charity. Liberty is not a vain word; it is the reign of God on earth, to the degree to which this can be realized. I believe firmly that, by natural and divine right, the nations belong only to themselves and that to make them the property of any man or class of men is a monstrous iniquity. I believe, finally, that these maxims, henceforward established in the human spirit, cannot be defeated and will sooner or later triumph, for in their triumph alone will be found the solution, sought in vain elsewhere, to the immense question of pauperism, on which depends the future fate of Humanity. Convinced, then, that nothing will stop the development of modern ideas, however one judges them, it seemed to me that it was important for the salvation of the people not to let them think that these ideas were opposed to Christianity on earth. I am all the more eager to fight such a damaging prejudice, since in my eyes the movement that is pulling the human race toward a new social situation, far from being contrary to the religion of Jesus Christ, is only its necessary effect, its political supplement, having been in preparation for eighteen centuries.

APPENDIX B

SELECTIONS FROM
LAMENNAIS' WRITINGS

(Translated from *Oeuvres complètes*.
2 vols. Brussels, 1839)

1. *From the Introduction to Volume I of the*
Essai sur l'indifférence en matière de religion

Society in Europe is advancing rapidly toward [a] fatal end. The grumblings in its midst, the blows that are shaking it, are not the most frightening symptom offered to the observer. But who will pull her from this lethargic indifference into which she is falling, this profound drowsiness? Who will breathe on these dry bones to reanimate them? Good and evil, the tree of life and that of death, nourished in the same soil, grow among the people, who, without raising their head, grasp their fruits at random. Religion, morality, honor, duty, the most sacred principles and most noble sentiments are now only a kind of dream, brilliant and supple phantoms who play for a moment in the background of one's thought, soon to disappear without return. No, never has anything like this been seen, even imagined. Long and persevering efforts were needed, a tireless struggle of man against his conscience and his reason, to attain this brutal carelessness. Rest your gaze for a moment on this king of creation: what incomprehensible degradation! His tired spirit is at ease only in the shadows. Ignorance is his joy, his felicity. He has even lost the desire to know what concerns him the most. Contemplating truth and error with equal disgust, he pretends to believe that they cannot be discerned, and mixes them in a common scorn. . . .

Truth is life, the sole cause of the existence of man and society.

Therefore, in the moral as in the political order, everything tends to destruction and advances toward this end more or less rapidly according to the fortunes and activity of the war against truth. A recent and too memorable experience leaves no doubt on this point. For anyone who is not blind, it is obvious that the French revolution, so eminently destructive, owed its character of death only to the impious delirium of its promoters, who attacked all truths together, with unprecedented rage.

Avenir articles

2. *October 16, 1830*

After thirty years of convulsions, of civil and foreign wars, of glory without and sorrow within, of anarchy and despotism, suddenly the shadow of the old royalty appeared and all eyes were fixed on this and people thought the order was going to return and that future repose was assured henceforth, for the monarchy brought words of peace and reconciliation. People talked of an eternal alliance concluded between the past and the present; and from the enormous ruins of I know not how many past governments a new edifice arose, a hastily constructed temple, in which the parties, renouncing their old hatreds, were to unite and fuse. All that happened yesterday, and today one would seek in vain some traces of what was regarded as affirmed forever; time rolls its floods over these vast ruins.

In less than a half century we have seen fall the absolute monarchy of Louis XIV, the republic of the convention, the directory, the consulate, the empire, the monarchy according to the Charter: what is durable? In this precipitous movement that sweeps people and their laws, institutions, and opinions, what remains, what survives deep in the hearts of men? Two things, only two things: God and liberty. Unite them, and all the intimate and permanent needs of human nature are satisfied; and calm reigns in the only area where it can reign on earth, in the area of the mind; separate them, and disorder begins immediately and increases until their union is effected once more.

The fever that agitates all the old Christian societies, the commotions that rock them, are only the reaction of Christianity itself against anarchy and despotism, to regenerate the world by re-establishing the order that has been progressively destroyed. And if this terrible fever is prolonged for a long time still, it is because a series of deplorable circumstances has agitated the very elements of life, religion and liberty.

When, after the tumults of the Fronde [civil war of 1648–1653], the last and weak effort of resistance to a government that would no longer recognize any limits, everything bent to the will of a single man, religion itself was enslaved and lost its dignity by losing its independence. The French clergy, despite the condemnations of Rome, received on its knees the servile doctrines that despotism insolently imposed upon it, corrupted in its own bosom the spirit of Catholicism, and, in the eyes of the people, rendered it the accomplice of the government that had pitched its tent on the last debris of Christian liberty. Finding servitude next to the altar, men grew frightened of God.

This cause among many others, produced the passionate philosophy of the eighteenth century, which simultaneously attacked despotism and religion, persuaded that neither could be defeated without overturning the other. When by a sudden, almost unanimous movement political emancipation was effected, the same opinion, established in the minds of some monsters, begat those frightful persecutions to which nothing in the annals of tyranny can be compared.

It is hardly surprising that from this came the long defiance of Catholics for anything that went under the name of liberty. This name revived in them too many sinister memories. It was too naturally confused in their mind with the hatred of Christianity for them not to fear it as the signal for the oppression of their dearest and most sacred rights. It must be admitted that little was done to disabuse them of this error, whose consequences, if it continues, will become more and more harmful.

Thus the two principles on which rest not only the happiness and the real improvement of people, but also their very existence, are now opposed.

Time, experience, and, it must be said to the honor of the century, serious and honest discussions have begun, on both sides, to diminish the prejudices. Already true liberalism, and this is incomparably the most prevalent type today, understands that liberty should be equal for all, or it is assured for no one; that Catholics have the same right to it as those who profess other doctrines; and that after all Catholicism— not the bastard and degenerate Catholicism of the Gallicans, but Roman Catholicism, which, by the admission of Protestants and the most enlightened Catholics, saved civilization and European liberty in the Middle Ages—has something noble and generous in it which no elevated spirit can ignore. We do not doubt that one day, by the progress of public reason, which frees itself year by year from the narrow prejudices and sad errors of the philosophy of the last century, it will be understood that not only does Catholicism have nothing incompatible with liberty but also it is in reality its only solid and durable base because, outside of it, liberty can never be more than a *fact*. But facts pass, only *right* remains; and when Catholicism is rejected, it is impossible for reason to conceive of right.

On the other side, Catholics, instructed by experience, have recognized that the government was a bad support for religion; that religion has its strength elsewhere, that is, in itself, and that its life is liberty. Stifled under the heavy protection of governments, the instrument of their politics and the toy of their whims, it would have perished if God, in the secret counsels of His providence, which ceaselessly watches over the only society that will not end, had not prepared its liberation. And the duty of Catholics is today to cooperate with all their power in this work of salvation and regeneration. For, after all, what can they desire if not the full and effective enjoyment of all the liberties that cannot legitimately be taken from any man: religious liberty, the liberty of education, and, in the civil and political order, the liberties protecting the security of person and property, along with the liberty of the press, which, we must not forget, is the strongest guarantee of all the others. To wish for anything else is to wish for the oppression of the Church and the ruin of the faith. This is what everyone should want, because it is the first interest of all men. This is the basis on which men sincerely attached to order can and should unite in good faith and without a hint of reticence.

There is, again, no need to be frightened of the novelty of this situation. Isn't everything new, unheard of, that has happened for forty years? There are exceptional epochs in which one should neither behave nor judge according to ordinary maxims and rules. When nothing is fixed in the world, neither the idea of right and of government, nor the idea of justice, nor even the idea of trust, one can escape a frightful series of tyrannies only by an immense development of individual liberty, which becomes the only possible guarantee of individual security, unless the social beliefs are reaffirmed and men's minds, dispersed, so to speak, in a limitless space, begin to gravitate toward a common center.

Let us seize eagerly on the portion of liberty that the laws grant us; and let us use it to conquer all that is due us, if we are refused it. We must not isolate ourselves and bury ourselves in a cowardly and stupid indolence. Catholics, let us learn to demand, to defend our rights, which are the rights of all Frenchmen, the rights of anyone who has resolved not to bow to any yoke, to reject all servitude, no matter what is title and what is disguise. We are free when we wish to be; we are free when we know how to unite and fight and die rather than yield the least portion of that which alone gives value to human life. There are temporary things, submitted to the inevitable vicissitudes of time, and there are eternal things; let us not confuse them. In the great shipwreck of the past, let us turn our gaze toward the future; it will be for us what we make of it. Let us rally frankly, completely, to any government that will maintain order and will legitimize itself by justice and respect for the rights of all. We ask no privileges of it; we ask liberty, offering it our strength in exchange. But let it be clear that if, in the wake of a blind passion, anyone dares try to impose chains upon us, we have sworn to break them on his head.

We have no hidden intentions, we have never had any; our word is our whole soul. Hoping then to be believed, we will say to those whose ideas differ, on many points, from our beliefs: if you sincerely wish religious liberty, the liberty of education (without which there is no religious liberty), you are one of ours; and we are yours also, for we wish no less sincerely, along with the liberty of the press, those political and civil liberties compatible with the maintenance of order. All liberties that the people can endure in the gradual development of their lives are due them, and their progress in civilization is measured by their real progress in liberty.

We are far from thinking that society has yet reached a stable situation. But if, before a harmony among its diverse elements is established, it is to endure new shocks, the union of those who are attached to true liberty will at least contribute to attenuate their violence and shorten their duration.

Let a sentiment of mutual love and tender compassion draw us all together despite our differences of opinions, soften the bitterness of our regrets, and gradually close the deep wounds that after all leave only honorable scars. We have all suffered in the various changes that have come so rapidly in the last half century. Our interests and affections have all been offended; complaints have been on all our lips and should enter all our hearts. Let us raise an altar to pity, and let its worship henceforth be sacred among us. Cursed be he who cannot find a tear for unspeakable misfortunes. But cursed be he who will not recognize the hand of God in these great catastrophes that confound human thought. And realities are often far from being what they seem, and the apparent rigor of celestial judgments often conceals immense compassion.

3. What Catholicism Will Be in the New Society, June 30, 1831

The character of truth, like that of justice, is to be essentially unchanging: religion, the perfect law of justice and truth, is therefore immutable in its essence. It cannot change any more than the nature of the beings whose relationships it expresses. But, while remaining always immutably the same, it is also in its nature to adopt different forms, either in the mind of man or in external society, to the extent that both develop under its influence. . . . Thus the Church, without really altering the principle and basis of its institutions, manifested itself in a different relationship with public society in the time of Charlemagne and his successors from that appropriate to its beginnings and to the centuries of persecution. In a word, the human spirit, by developing, penetrates increasingly the infinite depths of the divine truths, which do not change. And human society, by a similar progress, tends to become more and more spiritual, to draw closer and closer to the Church, which itself modifies its external forms, its manner of relation with society, in accordance with this progress. After having tried to establish the distinctive traits of this society that the world is trying to create, it will be useful and interesting to see what Catholicism will be in this new society and how the union of the two will be effected.

We have already said that science, long separated from faith, would be intimately allied with it: but we must conceive why this alliance will be necessarily effected and what results it will have. For every mind there exist two distinct elements of knowledge, both indispensable. One of these elements is the infinite itself, the pure idea of Being and what determines Being in itself. Without this idea there is no intelligence; for without it no proposition can be expounded, since every proposition involves the world "is," which assumes the pure, universal, and infinite idea of Being, which is the proper name for God. But for this idea to be grasped, it must be determined; therefore, the mind must include something that corresponds to what God or the infinite Being is in itself, to the properties that render it intelligible to itself. On the other hand, if the infinite is the original element of knowledge, relative to all created minds, it is not the only one; for all real knowledge takes a finite form in the human mind, insofar as it individually belongs to them. Moreover, if it is necessary that such minds know the infinite, that they know God in some way, in order to know anything at all, they also cannot know anything without knowing themselves, that is, without knowing the finite. And these two elements, the finite and the infinite, combine to form real intelligence and are found in all knowledge.

Hence the two modes of knowledge are naturally inseparable, although different and subordinate. Obviously the mind does not operate in the same way, does not sustain the same relations with the infinite and the finite. It perceives the first, without ever being able to embrace it entirely or to understand it; however, nothing in its nature prevents it from understanding or embracing the other entirely. The manner by which the mind knows or possesses the infinite is called faith; the manner by which it knows or possesses the finite is called conception, science. Science and faith are thus united by a natural and indissoluble link. No conception without faith, no faith without a beginning of conception, or science. The least religious philosophy necessarily has its dogmas or its objects of faith, just as religion has; but as it does not wish to relate them to their origin and as it tries to identify them with the objects of conception, it systematically confuses the finite and the infinite and creates a profound chaos of knowledge and even intelligence, within which the mind, in revolt against its own laws, is roused to a sterile and blind movement.

However, since the reason of all that is finite, of all that is contingent and relative, is found and can be found only in the infinite, in what is absolute and necessary, it follows that science has its reason and foundation in faith. And in fact science, which should be distinguished from the simple material observation of phenomena, has always borrowed its general character and the principles of its explanations from the dogmas of faith or from the notions that faith gives it of the infinite Being, of its necessary properties, of its mode of existence and of its own laws. Still today, anti-Christian science, unbelieving science, bases its theories only on notions of this type that are arbitrarily preconceived or implicitly admitted. But as none of these theories satisfies the whole range of problems that must be resolved by the explanation of their common and original causes, it is obviously led either to renounce all theory, that is, to destroy itself as real science, or to seek in other dogmas, more fruitful and more certain, the principle of its life and development.

On the other hand, Catholicism, toward the Middle Ages, had formed outside the facts, whose study was too long neglected, a science that men of great genius tried to deduce immediately from its dogmas. But, aside from the fact that the explicit knowledge of phenomena is indispensable to science, two factors prevented the success of this vast enterprise. First, men's minds, even the most powerful,

always circumscribed to some extent by the conceptions of their century, had not penetrated sufficiently into Catholic dogma to discover
and distinguish in it the universal laws of creation. For this is not the
fruit of one man's thought, but the successive work of society. Second,
the method that prevailed in the schools and that admitted only purely
logical procedures killed all invention by this alone, and could produce
only a verbal, abstract, and empty science.

Catholic science is therefore still to be created. This is what the
human mind is waiting for, tired of the insufficiency and disorder of
present science. From the certain notions of faith will spring, sooner
or later and perhaps sooner, a general system of explanation, a real
philosophy conforming to the needs of the times. This will be founded
on the constituent laws of intelligence and will return the different
orders of knowledge to unity, by showing that all orders are animated
in some manner by the same life and that the least exalted has its
reason and basis in the higher forms, and thus by uniting anew and
more tightly than ever that which always unites the nature of things,
belief and conception, God and the universe. From this harmony a
human but powerful proof of dogma will result; and rebel minds,
henceforth obliged to live both outside faith and outside science,
will return to Catholicism so that they will not perish.

The action of this new harmony will be great and healthy in another
respect. To the degree that society, based on increasing intelligence,
withdraws itself from the rule of force, which is the law of the brute,
this material link must be replaced by another, which will unite the
men whom liberty isolates and separates, and unite them voluntarily.
This link is no other than love; and since Catholicism, by its own
nature, develops liberty by developing the mind, it must develop love
proportionately. Otherwise, instead of perfecting society, it will destroy it. And in fact there is within Catholicism a principle of inexhaustible, immense love: love, the summary of the Law, is the whole
life of the Christian, his life in time and his life in eternity. The power
that Catholicism exercises in this respect over man, a power that its
most ardent enemies have not dared to contest and that struck the
founder of Islam with admiration, is manifest even in our epoch of
weakening faith. It would be beautiful to write a history of charity,
that is, of the most universal, pure, holy love in the Christian nations.
It could be seen fighting native ferocity in the Northern forests, soften-
ing the habits and laws there, producing the sentiment that we call
humanity, inspiring pity in the rich, tenderness for the poor, respect
for the weak in the powerful, bringing together all that interests,

prejudices, and pride divide, endowing tears with a divine force, elevating the rags of the indigent above the imperial purple, making a sublime dignity of suffering and misery, before which kings were ordered to fall to their knees. Never has this love ceased to flow from its imperishable source. Beneath the surface of egotism, with which the cold doctrines of a materialist philosophy have covered society, it has been able to penetrate, and to it is owed the increasing progress of that humanity and gentleness that characterize the people of Christ. In the liveliest exaltation of their hates and angers, the materialist doctrines show unprecedented horror of bloodshed. The spirit of persecution, relegated to a small number of men, is being extinguished and will soon yield entirely to the just ideas of liberty, which are spreading rapidly and which already prevail in public opinion. The last remnants of barbarism are gradually disappearing from legislation. No more torture and, soon one may hope, no more death penalty. Among the members of the same country, there is a visible tendency to associate and defend and protect one another. This tendency is manifested even more strikingly from people to people, in these new relations that are establishing an active and touching sympathy among the oppressed and unfortunate of all countries. Exclusive patriotism, the principle of so many calamities and crimes, is weakening and giving way to a generous sentiment of universal fraternity, which will diminish the causes of war and will make war itself less atrocious and disastrous. These are, certainly, great steps toward social improvement. What would happen, then, if Catholicism were entirely free and able, without impediment, to pour its ceaselessly renewed waves of love over this society, which is its work? Then we would see effaced in succession, insofar as this is possible on earth, whatever separates and divides individuals and nations who, freed politically and united among themselves by voluntary obedience to a single spiritual divine power, will live a powerful and common life. This is the love that created the human race, this is the love that saved it, and this is the love that, consummating its terrestrial unity, will show even here below a magnificent image of what the human race is destined to become in the other sphere.

The Church is the type and necessary means of this unity; it has called for it for eighteen centuries and works incessantly to realize it, to constitute this kingdom of Jesus Christ, who taught us to demand its advent from His Father. To be sure, much time will be necessary before it is established. We are only entering the period in which the last promises made to man by his redeemer are being accomplished.

However, already one can distinguish clearly the route on which the peoples are progressing; and although the intermediary points escape our gaze, faith and even reason easily discover the final goal. Freed from the chains that sovereignties had imposed upon it—sovereignties that must at least be profoundly modified if they are to be compatible with the new social order—the Church will become the firmest support of public liberties, which will be mingled with its own liberty; and it will become so not by the exercise of any political jurisdiction but by its internal and wholly spiritual strength. The revival of any power that would despoil the nations of their rights, so painfully acquired, would return the Church itself to servitude. Thus the Church will be increasingly identified with the people, who, above all, will render everything to it in gratitude and love. And if examples must be given of the possibility of such a union of the Church and the people, it would suffice to name Ireland, that noble land of faith and liberty.

It is a point of Catholic doctrine that the hierarchy, rising from the lower orders through the bishops to the sovereign pontiff, is of divine institution and therefore immutable. But it has existed in different forms in its relations with civil and political society. The first bishops, at the birth of Christianity, were different from those under the Greek emperors, who were different from those in the feudal monarchies, who were different still from those of the court monarchies. They have been invested, since Constantine, with numerous privileges, with a rank of State, men of government at the same time as they are men of God, surrounded with pomp and splendor. This sort of striking existence, and the power that was joined to it, could be useful in certain times and was really useful when the Church had to defend both its own independence and the rights of the weak entrusted to its guidance against brute force. But, obviously, nothing of this can continue. The mixture of the spiritual and the temporal was always, ultimately, harmful to religion; it will be manifestly impossible in societies where the government will be only the administration of material things and where each individual, administering his own affairs in full liberty, will have, by virtue of the same principle, the right to participate in the common affairs. How will the priest possess political privileges when there will be no political privileges for anyone? What can he ask or desire more than to be a citizen of his country by the same title as all the others, enjoying the same rights? Nevertheless, he will still have a great, a magnificent privilege, the privilege of devotion, the privilege of sacrifice; he cannot lose that, for he holds it from God. God has established him to be a man of the people, the confidant of the people's miseries, the doctor of its secret griefs, the depository of its sorrows, the interpreter of its needs, the protector, friend, father, the living providence of all those who are hungry and thirsty, all those who weep and have no one to console them. To suffer with them, to die for them, there is, again, the privilege of the priest; and he need yield this only if anyone ever disputes it.

The question of the poor is not only a question of political economy but also a question of life and death for society; because it is a life-and-death question for five-sixths of the human race, it is more than ever in Europe a question that calls for prompt solution. The ancients resolved it by slavery; the force of things would have resolved it in the same way in England, if Christianity, which has found a different solution there, for which humanity cannot be sufficiently grateful, had not posed an insurmountable barrier to the return of ancient servitude. It was not only by its spirit of mercy and charity that Christianity made possible the abolition of slavery, but also and especially by the manner in which it envisaged work, and by its institutions, which all tended to prevent the value of work from descending below certain limits. The Protestant spirit, which later became the philosophic spirit, on the contrary, tended to diminish the price of work indefinitely, to increase proportionately both the quantity of products and the profits on these products, and by this very fact it tends to increase steadily the distress of the poor and concentrate wealth in the hands of a small number of men, who traffic in the sweat of the poor and speculate on their hunger. It follows from this that unless there is a total change in the industrial system, a general rising of the poor against the rich will be inevitable and the entire society will be completely overturned and will perish in frightful convulsions. This is not the place to explain what Catholicism can and will do to remedy such great evils and prevent such terrible calamities. . . . I wish only to indicate here the immense career that will soon be open to the priest, called to serve, by new means, the suffering part of humanity. For whether agricultural colonies are developed (they have already been tried with success); or the principle of association is applied in industry to the profit of the poor; or, as is probable, industrial and agricultural work is united by a happy combination, the intervention of the priest will always be necessary, not only to give these associations the moral character on which their political utility and their material prosperity depend, but also so that a disinterested third party will serve as a link between the two parties of the contract, between the rich, who will furnish land and money, and the poor, who can put only his work in the common fund.

Yes, Catholicism will be great in the age that is beginning, in the age of liberty. Its ancient faith will fructify science, which will rely on it; the infinite love of which it is the source, by giving voluntary obedience as the basis for the new order, will revive the dignity of man, attenuate the causes of discord, make all peoples brothers, and make the whole human race what it originally was, a family. And "as there will always be the poor," they will be the family of the priest, his chosen children, whom he gathers and protects, because by reason of their sufferings and sorrows, their only heritage, the only one that they pass on, they are obviously the privileged of Christ, who was poor and suffering Himself, of the Christ who said: "Blessed are they who weep."

4. Suspension of the Avenir, November 15, 1831

A year ago, Catholics began a great battle, which, if they persevere, will end with the finest triumph ever granted to human efforts. The world will owe real liberty to them—not that false and destructive liberty that is traced with blood and that, after horrible devastation, succeeds in planting a sword on top of ruins; but a real liberty, founded on the respect for rights, inseparable from order, pure as the heaven from which it will receive its final development, holy like God, who has engraved an indelible desire for it in the heart of man. Then, and then only, Christianity, freed from the clouds that veil it, will appear once more on the horizon of society as the star that enlightens it, warms it, vivifies it; and the people, turning toward it, will accompany its magnificent course with their songs of joy and with eternally renewed hymns of their love. For it must not be ignored that if faith languishes, if religion inspires only disdain in many, it is because where governments hold it in bondage, it has lost in servitude its native character of grandeur and that whole vitality which, spreading its inexhaustible benefits, somehow followed our secret miseries to remedy them; it is because religion is impotent to defend the rights that Jesus Christ returned to the degenerate sons of Adam and instead of restoring its divine seal seems itself to bear the imprint of weakness and the decay of the chains that degrade it. Seeing religion as they have made it or as they have allowed it to be made, men have shrunk from this work of man.

But Catholics must not forget that they will not break these old chains in a single day. Everywhere human government tightens them convulsively in its grasp, persuaded that it cannot live if thought and conscience are free. But this grasp will loosen; already its strength is waning. That is why the government, foreseeing the end of its insolent domination over what has not been submitted to its rule, bends all its efforts to retain what is escaping it and to perpetuate its tyranny with a desperate effort. This is what is happening in France. The ministry tries to execute the Civil Constitution of the Clergy, by substituting itself for the people in the nomination of priests and bishops. It tries to control the temporal administration of the seminaries, while waiting to invade the spiritual administration by appointing directors and teachers. And it does not stop there: M. de Montalivet [the minister of education], in his intoxication with despotism, even feels authorized to designate the religious books that should be used in the primary schools of the [state] monopoly. He has come to believe that all the children in France belong to him, that it is up to him alone to regulate their faith, form their minds, in order to free the country from all *superstition*, and we know what this word means to him. The same measures, we can be sure, will be taken for all levels of teaching. They will even touch the bishops, for these must be dealt with in order to have done with *superstition*. Already deprived of the right to name the vicars general, the canons, the vicars who have their confidence, their mandaments, circulars and pastoral letters will be dictated, if the government has its way. Slaves even within their churches, they will be forced to leave them to make room for schismatics. And after having been reduced by police measures, they will be told harshly: return, we permit it. The ministry will prescribe even the details of worship; people will pray or not pray at a given hour as it will be pleased to order. What am I saying? I am not telling what will be, I am telling what is, what France can see, what rouses the indignation of any real man. No, no, the Catholics will not accept the infamous yoke that the state is trying to impose. They will crush this tyranny, and in its dust they will plant the liberty that will be their salvation and the salvation of the world. Too long they have bowed to the rod of their oppressors, too long they have slept the sleep of the slave. Let their reawakening mark as glorious an epoch in history as the rule of their tyrants is execrable and degrading for humanity. When their bold, powerful voice rises like a storm that breaks the bars of an old prison, it will reach even the old Christian heroes; and in the tombs where they rest, tired by work and by battle, their bones will stir.

And we who say this, we who call our brothers with all the force of our love for the holiest of causes, to the defense of what is to them, as to us, a thousand times dearer than life, will we abandon this sacred cause? Let God preserve us from such shame. If we retire for a moment, it is not from fatigue, still less from discouragement, it is to go, like the old soldiers of Israel, *to consult the Lord in Shiloh*. Our faith and our very intentions have been placed in doubt, for in these times everything is attacked. We quit the battlefield for a moment, to fulfill another, equally pressing duty. With a traveler's stick in hand, we make our way toward the eternal pulpit. There, prostrate at the feet of the pontiff whom Jesus Christ has set as guide and master for His disciples, we will say: O Father, deign to lower your glance to some of the last of your children who are accused of being rebels against your infallible and gentle authority; here they are before you; look in their souls, there is nothing they wish to hide; if even a single thought strays from yours they disavow it, they abjure it. You are the rule of their doctrines; never, no never have they known any other. O Father, pronounce over them the word that gives life, because it gives light, and let your hand extend to bless their obedience and their love.

5. *Words of a Believer*

To the People (from the Preface, 1835)

This book has been written primarily for you; it is to you that I offer it. May it cheer and console you a little amidst the many ills that afflict you, the many griefs that perpetually assail you.

For you who bear the daily burdens, I wish it could be to your poor, tired souls what the shade of the tree is in the corner of a field at midday, inadequate as this may be to those who have toiled all morning in the heat of the sun.

You are living in evil times, but these times will pass. After the hardships of winter, Providence returns a less rigorous season, and in its songs the tiny bird blesses the beneficent hand that has restored warmth and abundance to it, its mate and its cozy nest.

Hope and Love! Hope sweetens all things, and love makes them easy.

At the present time, there are people who suffer much because they love you greatly. I, their brother, have written the story of what they have done for you and of what has been done against them because of this; and when violence has died down, I will publish it, and you shall read it then with less bitter tears, and you too will love these men who have loved you so much.

At present, if I spoke to you of their love and their sufferings, I would be thrown in prison with them.

I would go there with great joy if I could relieve your misery a little thereby; but you would derive no benefit from it, and that is why we must wait and pray to God that He will shorten our trials.

Now it is men who judge and punish; soon He will judge. Happy the man who shall behold His justice.

I am old; listen to the words of an old man.

The earth is sad and parched, but it will become green again. The breath of the wicked will not forever pass over it like a burning wind.

Everything that happens is willed by Providence for your education, so that you will learn to be good and just when your hour comes. When those who abuse their power have been swept away before you like mud in streams on a stormy day, then you will understand that only the good endures, and you will fear to sully the air that the winds of heaven have purified.

Prepare your souls for this time, for it is not far off, it is drawing near.

Christ, crucified for you, has promised to deliver you.

Believe in His promise and, to hasten its realization, reform whatever needs reform in you; practice all the virtues; and love one another as the Savior of the human race has loved you, UNTO DEATH.

I

In the name of the Father, and of the Son, and of the Holy Ghost, Amen.

Glory to God in the heights of heaven, and peace on earth to men of good will.

Let he who has ears hear; let he who has eyes open them and see, for the time is coming.

The Father gave birth to the Son, His word, and the word was made flesh and lived among us; He came into the world and the world did not know Him.

The Son promised to send the consoling Spirit, the Spirit that proceeds from the Father and from Him; it will come and will renew the face of the earth, and this will be as a second creation.

Eighteen centuries ago, the Word spread the divine seed, and the Holy Spirit will fructify it. Men saw it flower and have tasted its fruits, fruits of the tree of life replanted in their humble dwelling.

I tell you, there was great joy among them when they saw the light appear and felt penetrated by a celestial fire.

Now the earth has become shadowy and cold once more.

Our fathers saw the sun set. When it dropped below the horizon, the whole human race trembled. Then there was something nameless in this night. Children of the night, the west is dark, but the east is beginning to grow light.

.   .   .   .

III

And I was borne in spirit to ancient times, when the earth was lovely and rich and fertile, and its inhabitants lived happily because they lived as brothers.

And I saw the Serpent gliding among them; it fixed its forceful gaze on several and their soul was troubled, and they drew close and the Serpent spoke to their ears.

And after having heard the word of the Serpent they rose and said: we are kings.

And the sun turned pale and the earth took on a funereal cast, like that of a shroud wrapping the dead.

And there was a dull murmur, a long wailing, and each man trembled in his heart.

In truth, I tell you, this was like the day the ocean burst its bounds and the great waters flooded in the Deluge.

Fear raced from hut to hut, for there were no palaces yet, and it said secret things to each man that made him shudder.

And those who had said, "We are kings," took a sword and followed Fear from hut to hut.

And strange mysteries occurred; there were chains and tears and blood.

Frightened men cried out: "Murder has reappeared in the world." And that was all, for Fear had benumbed their souls and deprived their arms of movement.

And they let themselves be fettered, and their wives and children as well.

And those who had said, "We are kings," dug a huge cavern and imprisoned the entire race there, just as animals are shut up in a barn.

And the storm chased the clouds and thunder rolled and I heard a voice saying: "The Serpent has won a second time, but not forever."

After that I heard nothing but confused voices, laughs, sobs, and blasphemies.

And I understood that there was to be a reign of Satan before the reign of God. And I wept, and hoped.

And the vision I saw was true: for the reign of Satan was established, and the reign of God will be established also; and those who said, "We are kings," will be shut up in the cavern with the Serpent in their turn, and the human race will come out. And this will be like another birth for it, like the passage from death to life. So be it!

.   .   .   .

VII

God made neither lowly nor great, masters nor slaves, kings nor subjects; He made all men equal. But among men, some have more strength or substance or spirit or will, and it is those who try to subject the rest, while pride and greed stifle in them the love of their brothers. And God knew that this would be, and that is why He commanded men to love one another, so that they might be united and the weak would not fall under the oppression of the strong. For he that is stronger than one alone is weaker than two, and he that is stronger than two is weaker than four; and so the weak will fear nothing when, loving one another, they shall be truly united.

.   .   .   .

IX

It is not that poverty comes from God, but it is a result of the corruption and evil greed of men, and that is why there are always poor. Poverty is the daughter of sin, the seed of which is in everyone, and of servitude, the seed of which is in every society. There will always be poor, because man will never destroy the sin within himself. There will always be less poor, because gradually servitude will disappear from society. If you wish to work to destroy poverty, work to destroy sin, first within yourself, then in others, and servitude in society.

It is not by taking from others that poverty can be destroyed. For, in creating poverty, how can one lessen the number of the poor? Everyone has a right to keep what he has; without this, no one would possess anything any more. But everyone has the right to acquire by his labor that which he lacks, without which poverty would be eternal.

So set free your labor, set free your arms, and poverty among men will no longer exist, save as an exception permitted by God, to remind men of the infirmity of their nature and the mutual help and love that they owe to one another.

.   .   .   .

XIII

It was a dark night; a starless sky weighed on the earth like a black marble lid on a tomb.

Nothing troubled the silence of the night save a strange noise like a light beating of wings, which could be heard above fields and cities.

And then the shadows thickened and each man felt his heart oppressed and a shudder ran through his veins.

And in a hall hung with black and lit by a reddish lamp, seven men dressed in purple, their heads encircled with crowns, were seated upon seven iron seats.

And in the middle of the hall rose a throne built with bones; at its base, as a footstool, was an inverted crucifix. In front of the throne was an ebony table, and on it a vase full of red, foaming blood, and a human skull.

The seven crowned men appeared pensive and sad, and from the depths of hollow sockets, their eyes from time to time flashed sparks of livid fire.

One of them got up and approached the throne with tottering steps, and set his foot upon the crucifix.

At this moment his limbs trembled and he seemed about to faint. The others looked at him without moving; they did not make the slightest gesture. But something passed over their brows and an inhuman smile contracted their lips.

The man who seemed about to faint extended his hand, seized the vase full of blood, poured some into the skull, and drank it.

The drink seemed to strengthen him.

He raised his head, this cry issuing from his chest like a hollow choking: "Cursed be Christ, who has restored liberty to earth."

And the six other crowned men all rose together and together uttered the same cry: "Cursed be Christ, who has restored liberty to earth."

After this, having sat down again on their iron chairs, the first man said: "My brothers, what will we do to stifle liberty: for our reign is ended if hers begins. Our cause is common: let each man suggest what seems best. Here is my advice. Before Christ came, who stood up to us? It is His religion that has ruined us. Let us abolish the religion of Christ."

Everyone answered: "It is true. Let us abolish the religion of Christ."

A second man advanced toward the throne, took the human skull, poured blood into it, drank it, and then said: "It is not only religion that we must abolish, but also science and thought. For science tries to learn things that it is not good for men to know, and thought is always ready to oppose force."

Everyone replied: "It is true. Let us abolish science and thought."

After having done what the first two had, a third man said: "When we have again plunged man into barbarism by taking religion, science, and thought from them, we will have accomplished a great deal, but there is still something left to do.

"A brute has dangerous instincts and sympathies. Let no people hear the voice of another people, lest if one complains and stirs, another might be tempted to imitate this. Let no sound from outside penetrate our domain."

Everyone replied: "It is true. Let no sound from outside penetrate our domain."

And a fourth said: "We have our interests and the people have theirs, contrary to ours. If they unite to defend this interest against us, how will we resist them?

"Let us divide and rule. Let us create in each province, each city, each village, an interest contrary to that of other villages, other cities, other provinces. By this means everyone will hate one another and they will not think of uniting against us."

Everyone replied: "It is true. Let us divide and rule. Harmony would destroy us."

A fifth man, having twice filled the skull with blood and twice emptied it, said: "I approve of all these methods, they are good, but insufficient. It is fine to create brutes, but frighten these brutes, strike them with terror by an inexorable justice and atrocious punishments, if you do not want to be destroyed sooner or later. The executioner is the first minister of a good prince."

And a sixth said: "I recognize the advantages of swift, terrible, inevitable punishments. But there are strong and desperate souls that endure tortures. If you want to govern men easily, soften them by luxury. Virtue is worth nothing to us, it begets strength; let us exhaust virtue by corruption."

Everyone answered: "It is true. Let us exhaust strength and energy and courage by corruption."

Then the seventh, having, like the rest, drunk from the human skull, spoke in this way, his feet on the crucifix: "No more Christ. There is deadly, eternal war between Him and us. But how are we to detach the people from Him? It is a vain effort. What should we do, then? Listen to me: we must win the priests of Christ with goods, honors, and power.

"They will order the people in Christ's name to be submissive to us in every matter, whatever we do or order.

"The people will believe them, and they will obey out of conscience, and our power will be stronger than before."

Everyone answered: "It is true. Let us win over the priests of Christ."

Suddenly the lamp that illuminated the room went out, and the seven men separated in the shadows.

And a voice said to a just man, who was at that moment watching and praying before the cross: "My day is coming. Adore, and fear nothing."

APPENDIX C

PAPAL STATEMENTS

1. From *Mirari vos* (August 15, 1832)
To all the Patriarchs, Prelates, Archbishops, and Bishops

God forbid, dear Brothers, that pastors might fail their duty because of so many evils and dangers or that, out of fear, they might abandon the care of their flock or rest in cowardly repose. Let us defend our common cause, or rather the cause of God, in the unity of a single spirit and let us join our vigilance and efforts against the common enemy for the salvation of the whole people.

You will fulfill this duty if, as your office demands, you watch over yourselves and over doctrine, recalling ceaselessly that the universal Church is shaken by any novelty whatsoever and that, as the pope Saint Agathon stated, "nothing that has been defined should be retracted or changed or supplemented" but that "both the meaning and the expression should be kept pure." So let the unity based on the chair of Saint Peter be firm and unshakable. From this will flow for all churches the advantages of a precious communion. In this all will find a rampart, a sure refuge, a port amid storms, and a treasury of numberless riches. Thus, to repress the audacity of those who try to limit the rights of the Holy See or to break the union of the churches with this See, a union which alone sustains them and gives them life, inculcate a great zeal; a sincere veneration and confidence for this eminent Chair. . . .

You should then work and watch ceaselessly to preserve the depository of faith amid that impious conspiracy which we see with sorrow attempting to ravage and destroy it. Let everyone remember that the judgment on the holy doctrine by which the people should be taught and on the government of the whole Church belongs to the Roman pontiff. . . . It is the duty of every bishop to attach himself loyally to the chair of Peter, to preserve the faith religiously and to govern the flock entrusted to him. It is the duty of priests to be submitted to the bishops, whom Saint Jerome advises them to "consider the fathers of their souls"; they should never forget that the canons forbid them to do anything in the ministry or to assume the power of teaching and preaching "without the permission of the bishop, to whose faith the people are entrusted and of whom the accounting of the care of souls is required." Let it thus remain certain that all those who undertake anything against this established order are troubling the state of the Church as much as it is their power to do.

It would doubtless be culpable and entirely contrary to the respect with which the laws of the Church should be received to criticize by a mad disorder of opinions the discipline established by the Church, which includes the administration of the holy things, the regulation of morals, and the rights of the Church and its ministers; or to claim that this discipline is opposed to the certain principles of the law of nature or to present it as defective, imperfect, or submitted to the civil authority.

As it is invariable, to use the words of the Fathers of Trent, that the Church "has been instructed by Jesus Christ and his apostles and that it is informed by the Holy Spirit which constantly instills every truth," it is completely absurd and eminently insulting for anyone to hold that a "restoration" or "regeneration" is necessary to preserve and increase the Church; as if it could be judged open to failure or ignorance or to other drawbacks of this nature. The goal of the innovators, in this, is to lay the foundations for a new human institution, and . . . to make the Church, which is divine, wholly human. Let those who form such plans remember that it is to the Roman pontiff alone, according to the testimony of Saint Leo, that the dispensation of the canons has been entrusted, and that it is his duty alone, not that of any individual, to pronounce on the ancient rules. . . .

We arrive now at another cause of the evils with which the Church is lamentably afflicted at this moment, to wit, this *indifference* or perverse opinion that has been spread so widely by the tricks of evil men, according to which a man can gain eternal salvation by any profession of any faith, provided that his morals are correct and honest. It should not be difficult for you to reject such a fatal error in such a clear and evident matter, among the people confided to your care. Since the apostle cautions us that "there is only one God, one

faith, one baptism" . . . there is no doubt that they will perish eternally
if they do not hold to the Catholic faith and keep it entire and
inviolable. . . .

From this corrupted source of indifference comes that absurd and
erroneous maxim, or rather that madness, that it is necessary to assure
and guarantee liberty of conscience to everyone. The way is prepared
for this pernicious error by the full and limitless liberty of opinions
which is spread to the disadvantage of religious and civil society,
though some people repeat with extreme impudence that some gain
results for religion from this. But, Saint Augustine said, "what can
more easily give death to the soul than the liberty of error?" In effect,
when every restraint which can maintain men in the path of truth is
taken away, their nature, inclined to evil, falls into an abyss; and we
can say with truth that the "well of the abyss" is opened. . . . From
this stem the change in men's minds, the deep corruption of youth, the
scorn for holy matters and the most respectable laws which has spread
among the people, in a word the most fatal scourge for society, since
experience from remote antiquity has shown that the States which
have glittered by their wealth, their power, and their glory, have perished by this simple evil, the immoderate liberty of opinions, the
license for speech and the love of novelties.

Related to this is that fatal liberty, which cannot be sufficiently
feared—the liberty of the press to publish any writing whatsoever, a
liberty which some people dare to solicit and extend with so much
zeal. We are frightened, venerable Brothers, at the thought of the
doctrines, or rather the monstrous errors, with which we are over-
whelmed, realizing that they are spread everywhere, by a multitude of
books and by publications of all sorts. . . . There are those, however,
who are led to such a degree of impudence that they maintain stubbornly that the flood of errors which results from this is sufficiently
compensated by one book which, amid this mass of perversity, appears
to defend religion and truth. But this is surely a forbidden thing,
contrary to all notions of equity, to allow, by premeditation, a certain
and greater evil because there is a hope that some good will result.
What man in his right mind would say that poisons should be allowed
to spread freely, to be sold and transported publicly, even to be drunk,
because there is a remedy that might sometimes save those who use it
from death? . . .

According to the constant care with which the Holy See has tried at
all times to condemn suspect and harmful books and to withdraw
them from the hands of the faithful, it is obvious how false, brash,

insulting to the Holy See and harmful for the Christian people this doctrine is, the doctrine of those who not only reject the censorship of books as an unduly onerous yoke but who go to the dishonest extreme of presenting it as opposed to the principles of right and justice and daring to refuse to the Church the right to order and exercise it.

As we have learned that some writings spread among the people proclaim certain doctrines which shake the loyalty and submission owed to princes, and which kindle the spark of revolt, we must carefully prevent the people from being drawn outside the path of duty. . . . Divine and human laws oppose those who try to shake the loyalty to princes and cast them from their thrones, by the shameful plots of revolt and sedition. . . .

[The] beautiful examples of ineradicable submission to the princes, which are a necessary consequence of the holy precepts of the Christian religion, condemn the detestable insolence and evil of those who, inflamed with immoderate zeal for a rash liberty, try with all their strength to disturb and overturn all the rights of governments, while basically they bring to the people only servitude under the mask of liberty. . . . These cheats . . . aspire to the boast of Luther of being free with regard to everyone and, to achieve this more easily and quickly, boldly attempt the most criminal enterprises.

We could foresee no good for religion and for governments if we followed the wishes of those who desire the separation of Church and State and the breaking of the mutual harmony of secular and priestly rule. For it is certain that this harmony, which was always so favorable and so salutary to the interests both of religion and of the civil authority, is feared by the partisans of a limitless liberty.

To the other causes of bitterness and worry which principally torment and afflict us in the general danger, are added certain notable associations and meetings in which common cause is made with people of every religion, even false ones, where respect for religion is feigned but really, from the thirst for novelty and to arouse seditions everywhere, all kinds of liberty are urged, disorders against the good of Church and State are aroused, and the most respectable authorities destroyed.

It is certainly with sorrow, but also with confidence in Him who commands the winds and restores calm, that we write you all this, venerable Brothers, so that you may don the shield of faith and strive to fight courageously for the Lord. It is your duty above all to stand as a rampart against any pride that rises against the truth of God. Draw the sword of the spirit which is the word of God and let those who hunger for justice receive from you the bread of this word. You are called to be diligent workers in the vineyards of the Lord; devote yourselves to planning and working together to remove from the field entrusted to you every bitter root, to stifle every vicious seed, and to cultivate an abundant harvest of virtues. Embracing in your paternal affection those who apply themselves to ecclesiastical studies and questions of philosophy, exhort them firmly not to rely imprudently on their minds alone, which would divert them from the path of truth and draw them into the course of the impious. Let them remember that God is the "guide of wisdom" and the "corrector of the wise," and that we cannot know God without God, who teaches men by his Word to know God. Only a proud or rather a mad man weighs in a human scale the mysteries of the faith which surpass all understanding, and relies on our reason, which is weak by the very condition of human nature.

Let our dear children in Christ, the princes, favor by their aid and authority these wishes which we express for the salvation of religion and the State. Let them consider that their authority has been given not only for temporal government but especially to defend the Church, and that everything that is done for the good of the Church is done also for their power and security. Let them realize even that the cause of religion should be dearer to them than that of the throne. . . . Placed as fathers and tutors of the people, they procure for them a true, constant, and prosperous peace and tranquillity if they devote themselves to maintaining religion and piety toward God. . . .

2. Singulari nos (July 7, 1834)
Encyclical letter to all the Patriarchs, Prelates, Archbishops, and Bishops

Venerable Brothers, greetings and apostolic blessings.

We felt a real joy over the striking testimonies of faith, obedience, and religion with which we learn that people everywhere hastened to welcome our Encyclical of August 15, 1832, in which, to accomplish the duty of our office, we announced to the whole Catholic flock the holy doctrine, the only doctrine which can be followed on each of the points dealt with in it. Our joy was increased by the declarations which were given on this subject by some of those who had approved the beliefs and systems of which we complained and had aided and defended them. We recognized, it is true, that the evil had not yet disappeared, and the publication of little writings full of imprudence and some shady plots clearly revealed that the evil continued, to combat the interests both of religion and of the States. Thus we expressed our deep disapproval in the letter written, in the month of October, to our venerable brother the bishop of Rennes. But while we were worried and while this affair inspired lively concern, it was fine and pleasant to receive from the man who was the principal cause of our grief, a declaration of December 11 in which he assured in clear and formal terms that he followed solely and absolutely the doctrine taught in our Encyclical and that he would write and approve nothing that was contrary to it. Immediately we extended our paternal charity to this son, whom we believed sufficiently touched by our warnings to hope that he would give us increasingly firm evidence that he was submitted to our judgment, openly and in his heart.

However, though it seemed scarcely believable, the man whom we had treated with such a generous sentiment, forgetting our indulgence, quickly abandoned his resolution, and the hope that we had nourished of the "fruit of our teaching" was completely lost, as soon as we learned that he had, anonymously to be sure but with an anonymity belied by public statements, published and spread everywhere a book in the French language, slight in its volume but immense in its perversity, called: *Paroles d'un Croyant.*

We were truly seized with horror, venerable Brothers, at our first glance at this book; and, moved by compassion for the blindness of its author, we understood what excesses are produced by a science which is not of God but of the spirit of this world. In effect, scorning the vow solemnly given in his declaration, he undertook, covered as usual by cunning words and fictions, to shake and destroy Catholic doctrine as, by virtue of the authority entrusted to our weaknesses, we defined it in the Encyclical already cited, on matters of the submission owed to governments and on the obligation to turn the people from the pernicious scourge of indifference and to restrain the limitless license of speech and opinions and, finally, on the absolute liberty of conscience, a completely condemned liberty, and on this horrible conspiracy of societies composed of partisans of all the false religions and all the sects for the ruin of the church and the State.

The mind is truly shocked to read just the pages of this book in which the author tries to break all the bonds of loyalty and submission toward the princes and, spreading everywhere the sparks of sedition and revolt, extends the destruction of public order, disrespect for the magistrates, violation of the laws, and undermines the very foundations of all religious and civil government. Then, in a series of unjust and unheard-of assertions, in a mass of calumnies, he portrays the power of princes as contrary to divine laws, even as the work of sin, as the result of Satan himself, and he blasts with the same tone of infamy those who preside over divine things and the leaders of States, because of an alliance of crimes and plots which he imagines has been concluded between them against the rights of the people. Not satisfied with such great audacity, he wishes to establish by violence the absolute liberty of opinions, of speech, and of conscience; he wishes every success to those who battle to establish this liberty from tyranny (this is the word he uses); in the excess of his rage he incites the people to unite and associate in all parts of the world and he ceaselessly urges and presses toward the realization of such pernicious plans that we feel that, on this matter too, he is violating our warnings and our regulations.

It grieves us to recall here everything that conspired in this detestable production of impiety and audacity to produce the upheaval of divine and human matters. But what particularly arouses indignation, what religion can absolutely not endure, is the fact that the author, to confirm such grave mistakes, uses and repeats with a confidence which deludes the imprudent, the teachings of God Himself; it is a fact that to free the people from the law of obedience, as it is conveyed and inspired by God, he begins in the name of the August and very holy Trinity and then everywhere cites the holy Scriptures and distorts their words, the words of God, from their real meaning, using them astutely and boldly to inculcate the dangerous ravings of his imagination, hoping thus, as Saint Bernard said, more certainly to put shadows in the place of light and serve poison instead of honey or rather in honey itself, constructing a new Bible for the people and setting a different foundation from that which has been constructed.

To ignore by our silence such a dangerous blow to holy doctrine is forbidden by Him who has placed us like the guards in Israel, to warn against error those people whom the author and perfector of our faith, Jesus Christ, has entrusted to our care.

This is why, after having heard some of our venerable brothers, the cardinals of the holy Roman Church, of our own volition and certain knowledge and from the whole plenitude of our apostolic power, we disapprove, condemn, and decree that it be held disapproved and condemned in perpetuity, the book of which we have just spoken, which is entitled: *Paroles d'un Croyant,* in which, by an impious abuse of the word of God, the people are criminally incited to break the bonds of all public order, to overturn every authority, to arouse, sustain, extend, and fortify seditions, disorders, and rebellions in the states; a book including consequently propositions respectively false, calumnious, rash, leading to anarchy, contrary to the word of God, impious, scandalous, erroneous, already condemned by the Church, especially in the Waldensians, the Wycliffites, the Hussites, and other heretics of this kind.

It will now be your duty, venerable Brothers, to support this decision of our authority with all your efforts, which the salvation and the preservation of the Church as well as of the State demand, so that this book, conceived in the shadows for the ruin of societies, does not become still more pernicious and encourage even more the limitless desires of a mad novelty and spread like a cancer among the people. Let it be a duty for you tirelessly to spread the holy doctrine on such an important point, to reveal the tricks of the innovators, and to watch over the flock with more zeal than ever, so that study of religion, piety in actions, and public peace may flourish and spread. This is what we confidently expect of your faith and your indefatigable ardor for the common good; so that with the aid of Him who is the father of light, we can rejoice (as Saint Cyprien said) that "error has been understood and repressed" and that it has been confounded by the fact that "it has been recognized and revealed."

Besides, it is really deplorable to see the extremes of madness in which human reason indulges, when a man yields to the love of novelty and, despite the warnings of the apostle, trying to be "wiser than he should," too confident in himself, thinks that he should seek the truth outside the Catholic Church, where it is found without the impure admixture of even the slightest error, and which is thus called and really is the foundation and the unshakable support of the truth. You readily understand, venerable Brothers, that here we speak also of this fallacious system of philosophy which has been recently invented and which we must entirely disapprove, a system in which, drawn by a rash and unrestrained love of novelties, truth is no longer sought where it is with certainty, but where, disregarding the holy and apostolic traditions, other vain, futile, and uncertain doctrines are introduced, which are not approved by the Church, and on which the most vain men falsely think that the truth can be established and supported.

But while we write these things to satisfy the full duty of care and vigilance which God has imposed on us, to know, define, and preserve the holy doctrine, we bemoan the grievous wound which the error of our son has caused in our heart, and, in the extreme affliction with which it burdens us, there remains only one hope of consolation, to see him return to the paths of justice. Therefore let us raise our eyes and hands together toward Heaven, "which directs and corrects the wise." Let us pray urgently to give him a docile heart and a generous soul, so that he may hear the voice of the most tender and afflicted father, and that there may come from him as soon as possible those things which constitute the joy of the Church, the joy of your ranks, the joy of the Holy See, our own joy who are placed there despite our weakness. Surely it will be a beautiful and happy day for us when we can welcome this son, restored to himself, to our paternal bosom, when he will give us by his example the best reason to hope for the return to repentance of those whom he may have drawn into his error, so that, for the good of the Church and of the States, there is in everyone a single manner of viewing the doctrines, a single goal in all undertakings, a perfect harmony in behavior and beliefs. We seek and expect from your pastoral care that you will request this great good from God, as we will, by your wishes and your prayers. Imploring heavenly aid for this purpose, we grant you and your flock as a pledge, with the liveliest affection, the apostolic blessing.

Given at Saint Peter of Rome, the VII calend of July, the year 1834 and the fourth year of our pontificate.

GREGORY XVI, Pope

NOTES

CHAPTER II. LAMENNAIS AND THE CHURCH TO 1815

1. Charles Boutard, *Lamennais, sa vie et ses doctrines* (Paris, 1913), I, 281–2.
2. Boutard, I, 124.
3. Boutard, I, 23.
4. Anatole Feugère, *Lamennais avant l'essai sur l'indifférence* (Paris, 1906), p. 242.

CHAPTER III. LAMENNAIS AND THE CHURCH IN THE RESTORATION

1. Adrien Dansette, *Histoire religieuse de la France contemporaine* (Paris, 1948), I, 240.
2. Félicité de Lamennais, *Essai sur l'Indifférence en Matière de Religion* (Paris, 1828), I, 50.
3. Félicité de Lamennais, "Lettres inédites à J. Saint-Victor," ed. Louis Barthous, *Revue des Deux Mondes* (November 1923), XVIII, 177. Letter of February 25, 1820.
4. Boutard, I, 310.
5. Félicité de Lamennais, *Oeuvres complètes* (Brussels, 1839), II, 77.
6. Claude Carcopino, *Les doctrines sociales de Lamennais* (Paris, 1942), pp. 80–1.
7. Boutard, I, 379.
8. Alec R. Vidler, *Prophecy and Papacy* (London, 1954), p. 123.
9. Félicité de Lamennais, *Correspondance*, ed. Emile Forgues (Paris, 1864), I, 283. Letter of December 27, 1827.

10. Lamennais, *Oeuvres complètes*, II, 290.

11. Boutard, II, 53.

12. Lamennais, *Correspondance*, II, 148. Letter of June 16, 1830.

13. R. Combalot, *Deuxième lettre à M. F. de La Mennais en réponse à son livre contre Rome intitulé "Affaires de Rome"* (Paris, 1837), p. 179.

14. Louis Veuillot, "Charles Sainte-Foi," *Revue du Monde Catholique* (December 1861), II, 357–69.

15. Jean Pictave, "La Separation de Lacordaire et de La Mennais," *La Vie intellectuelle* (December 1932), XVIII, 187.

16. Henri-Dominique Lacordaire, *Lettres à Théophile Foisset*, ed. Joseph Crépon (Paris, 1886), I, 191. Letter of July 1830. Henri-Dominique Lacordaire, *Le Testament du P. Lacordaire*, ed. Charles Comte de Montalembert (Paris, 1870), p. 51.

17. F. Duine, *Essai de Bibliographie de Félicité Robert de la Mennais* (Paris, 1923), p. v.

18. Lamennais, *Correspondance*, II, 166. Letter of December 24, 1829.

19. Félicité de Lamennais, *Le Prêtre et l'ami: Lettres inédites à la Baronne Cottu*, ed. Comte d'Haussonville (Paris, 1910), p. 219.

CHAPTER IV. THE "AVENIR" MOVEMENT

1. John M. S. Allison, *Church and State in the Reign of Louis-Philippe* (Princeton, 1916), p. 26.

2. Boutard, II, 117. Letter of August 26, 1830.

3. Lamennais, *Correspondance*, II, 167. Letter of August 27, 1830.

4. *Ibid.*, II, 171. Letter of September 20, 1830.

5. Olympe-Philippe Gerbet, "Un disciple. Lettres inédites à Lamennais," *Revue Britannique* (July 1885), IV, 108.

6. Charles de Montalembert, "Lettres à Gustave Lemarcis," ed. Victor Bucaille, *Revue Montalembert* (1910), III, 628–9. Letter of November 24, 1830.

7. Boutard, II, 118. Letter of August 27, 1830.

8. Lamennais, *Correspondance*, II, 217. Letter of June 26, 1831.

9. *L'Avenir*, October 16, 1830.

10. *L'Avenir*, January 31, 1831.

11. *L'Avenir*, October 16, 1830.

12. *L'Avenir*, October 18, 1830. By Lamennais.

13. *L'Avenir*, October 17, 1830.

14. *L'Avenir*, February 8, 1831.

15. *L'Avenir*, November 27, 1830. By Lamennais.
16. *L'Avenir*, February 18, 1831. By Lamennais.
17. *L'Avenir*, March 3, 1831.
18. *L'Avenir*, April 26, 1831.
19. *L'Avenir*, February 22, 1831.
20. *L'Avenir*, November 15, 1831.
21. Boutard, II, 263.
22. Lamennais, *Correspondance*, II, 189. Letter of December 23, 1830.

CHAPTER V. RESPONSE TO THE "AVENIR"

1. *Ibid.*, II, 25. Letter of December 5, 1830.
2. Boutard, II, 243.
3. *L'Avenir*, October 27, 1831. Article from a liberal paper, *Le Dauphinois*.
4. P. de Lallemand, *Montalembert et ses amis dans le romanticisme* (Paris, 1927), p. 60.
5. Montalembert, "Lettres à Lemarcis," p. 625.
6. *L'Avenir*, May 6, 1831.
7. Lamennais, *Correspondance*, II, 251 and 312. Letters of December 5, 1830, and November 8, 1831.
8. *Le Courrier français*, October 19, 1830.
9. *Le Courrier français*, November 28, 1830.
10. *L'Avenir*, September 5, 1831. Article from *Le Courrier français*.
11. Vidler, p. 186.
12. Archives nationales, F[18]318. Letter from Paris prefect of police to the Minister of Commerce, August 17, 1831.
13. *L'Avenir*, September 5, 1831.
14. *Ami de la Religion*, May 26, 1831. Letter from the Archbishop of Besançon.
15. Vrindts, *Les Erreurs de l'abbé de Lamennais à l'occasion de son recours inutile et intempestif à Rome* (Brussels, 1832), p. 113.
16. Monsignor Guillon, *Histoire de la nouvelle hérésie du XIXe siècle* (Paris, 1835), II, 491.
17. Lamennais, *Correspondance*, II, 312. Letter of November 8, 1831.
18. *Ami de la Religion*, February 19, 1831.
19. *Ami de la Religion*, November 5, 1831.
20. *L'Avenir*, April 29, 1831. By Lamennais.
21. Lamennais, *Correspondance*, II, 312. Letter of November 8, 1831.
22. Lecanuet, *Montalembert; Sa Jeunesse* (Paris, 1895), p. 267.

23. Félicité de Lamennais, *Lamennais et ses correspondants inconnus,* ed. Alfred Roussel (Paris, 1912), p. 357.

CHAPTER VI. LAMENNAIS AND GREGORY XVI

1. Dansette, I, 306.
2. Lamennais, *Correspondance,* II, 402. Letter of April, 1834.
3. Liselotte Ahrens, *Lamennais und Deutschland* (Münster, 1930), p. 267.

POSTSCRIPT

1. Victor Giraud, *La Vie tragique de Lamennais* (Paris, 1933), p. 170.
2. *Ibid.,* 170.

BIBLIOGRAPHICAL ESSAY

There are many sources for a study of Lamennais. Lamennais himself was a prolific writer, of letters as well as of formal works. Several of his colleagues wrote voluminously also. There is a wealth of contemporary comment on the Mennaisian movement, mostly hostile. The whole movement has been extensively studied by historians, particularly from a biographical point of view. Much of this work has been poorly done. Many studies have utilized few of the available source materials. Many writers have adopted an antiquarian rather than a historical view, failing to establish an adequate historical framework for the subject. And the whole problem has aroused much partisan treatment by French scholars. Up to quite recent years, the desire to attack the Church or French liberalism through a study of Lamennais has dominated much of the literature.

Even on qualitative grounds, then, there is no need to cite more than a fraction of the relevant publications. The quantity of the material defies a complete listing in the present essay. Still, there is ample room for those who wish to pursue the main problems further. The following references are intended to provide initial guidance for more detailed work and to indicate some of the main sources used in this essay.

There is elaborate and interesting primary material from Lamennais and his collaborators. The *Agence générale pour la défense de la liberté religieuse* issued a number of pamphlets. It published also the *Mélanges Catholiques: Extraits de l'Avenir* (2 vols., Paris, 1831), an excellent collection of the leading articles of the paper. The *Avenir* itself is available, as are the *Mémorial Catholique* and the *Revue Catholique*.

Lamennais' collected works were published several times. The most convenient, for writings through 1834, is the *Oeuvres complètes* issued in two volumes in Brussels in 1839. Lamennais' separate publications are available also, in various editions. Aside from *Essai sur l'Indifférence*, only *Paroles d'un Croyant* has been translated from the period before 1834; the 1834 translation published in London is best, but there is a more recent one, also from London, of 1942. The principal collections of letters are *Correspondance*, ed. Emile D. Forgues (2 vols., Paris, 1864); *Correspondance inédite entre Lamennais et le Baron de Vitrolles*, ed. Eugène Forgues (Paris, 1886); *Lettres inédites à Montalembert*, ed. Eugène Forgues (Paris, 1898); *Un Lamennais Inconnu*, ed. August Laveille (Paris, 1898); and *Oeuvres inédites*, ed. Agne Blaize (2 vols., Paris, 1866). These collections and others give excellent insight into Lamennais' thinking, even if they seldom reveal much of his personality. For a general bibliography of works by and about Lamennais, see Hector Talvart and Joseph Place, *Bibliographie des Auteurs Modernes de Langue Française* (Paris, 1952), VII, 357–62; X, 307–40; XI, 167–229. See also F. Duine, *Essaie de Bibliographie de Félicité Robert de La Mennais* (Paris, 1923).

For Lacordaire's works, see *Le Testament du P. Lacordaire*, ed. Charles Comte de Montalembert (Paris, 1870); *Lettres à Théophile Foisset*, ed. Joseph Crépon (Vol. I, Paris, 1886); and *Oeuvres philosophiques et politiques* (Paris, 1872). For the writings of Montalembert, see Adam Mickiewicz, *Livre des Pèlerins Polonais*, trans. Comte Charles de Montalembert (Paris, 1834); *Le Père Lacordaire* (Paris, 1862); *Lettres à Lamennais*, eds. Georges Goyau and P. Lallemand (Paris, 1932); and *Lettres à un Ami de Collège, 1827-1830* (Paris, 1884).

For contemporary reactions to the movement, see *L'Ami de la Religion*, 1830-1834; Abbé Boyer, *Examen de la Doctrine de M. de La Mennais* (Paris, 1834); *Documents Mennaisiens*, ed. F. Duine (Paris, 1919); *Le Portefeuille de Lamennais*, ed. Georges Goyau (Paris, 1930).

The best study of the July Monarchy remains Sébastien Charléty, *La Monarchie de juillet* (Paris, 1922); for the Restoration, see Charléty, *La Restauration* (Paris, 1921), and G. de Bertier de Sauvigny, *La Restauration* (Paris, 1955). In English, J. Lucas-Dubreton, *The Restoration and the July Monarchy* (New York, 1929), is the best available.

There are several good studies of Church-state relations in the modern period. John M. S. Allison, *Church and State in the Reign of Louis-Philippe* (Princeton, 1916), provides an adequate factual summary. The most valuable book is by Adrien Dansette, *Histoire religieuse de la France contemporaine* (Vol. I, Paris, 1948), which has been badly translated as *Religious History of Modern France* (Freiburg, 1961). A. Débidour, *Histoire des rapports de l'église et de l'état en France* (Paris, 1898), gives a classic anticlerical view. Paul Droulers, *Action pastorale et problèmes sociaux sous la monarchie de juillet chez Mgr. d'Astros, archévêque de Toulouse, censeur de La Mennais* (Paris, 1954), offers insight into the French hierarchy. Henri Haag, *Les Origines du Catholicisme libéral en Belgique* (Louvain, 1950), is excellent. L. S. Phillips, *The Church in France* (London, 1929), is the best survey in English. Georges Weill, *Histoire au Catholicisme libéral en France* (Paris, 1909), remains unsurpassed.

For the Church more generally, see Liselotte Ahrens, *Lamennais und Deutschland* (Münster, 1930), for an account of the diplomatic pressures on the pope. Jean Leflon, *La Crise révolutionnaire, 1789-1848*, Vol. XX, in *Histoire de l'Église* (Paris, 1949), is a fine general study. In English, for both France and the papacy, see Joseph N. Moody, *Church and Society* (New York, 1953). See also E. L. Woodward, *Three Studies in European Conservatism* (London, 1929).

Of the many biographies of Lamennais, the most comprehensive is Charles Boutard, *Lamennais, sa vie et ses doctrines* (3 vols., Paris, 1913 ff.). Etienne Cabanès, *Grands névropathes* (Vol. II, Paris, 1931), offers an attempt at psychoanalysis. For polemics, see Robert Havard de la Montagne, *Histoire de la Démocratie chrétienne* (Paris, n.d.), for a recent, hostile view of Lamennais, and E. Spuller, *Lamennais* (Paris, 1892), for a favorable verdict. Finally, Alec R. Vidler, *Prophecy and Papacy* (London, 1954), offers an excellent treatment in English.

Two biographies of Lacordaire are worth noting. One, very sympathetic, is by his friend Théophile Foisset, *Vie du R. P. Lacordaire* (2 vols., Paris, 1870); the other is by L. C. Sheppard, *Lacordaire, a biographical essay* (New York, 1964). The standard work on Montalembert is Lecanuet, *Montalembert, Sa Jeunesse* (Paris, 1895). Also useful is André Trannoy, *Le Romanticisme politique de Montalembert avant 1843* (Paris, 1942). Biographies of other Mennaisians are very poor.

Dansette and Phillips provide the best studies of the context of the *Avenir* movement. Boutard, Trannoy, and Vidler offer the best insights into the movement itself, and into the character of Lamennais. Beyond these works, the abundance of articles, letters, and other publications by Lamennais and his collaborators allows direct study of the abortive effort to modernize the Church.

INDEX